CHANAKYA'S
7 SECRETS *of* LEADERSHIP

CHANAKYA'S 7 SECRETS *of* LEADERSHIP

Radhakrishnan Pillai

National bestselling author of *Corporate Chanakya*

D. Sivanandhan

Former Commissioner of Police, Mumbai &
Director General of Police, Maharashtra

JAICO PUBLISHING HOUSE

Ahmedabad Bangalore Bhopal Bhubaneswar Chennai
Delhi Hyderabad Kolkata Lucknow Mumbai

Published by Jaico Publishing House
A-2 Jash Chambers, 7-A Sir Phirozshah Mehta Road
Fort, Mumbai - 400 001
jaicopub@jaicobooks.com
www.jaicobooks.com

CHANAKYA'S 7 SECRETS OF LEADERSHIP
ISBN 978-81-8495-401-2

First Jaico Impression: 2014
Twenty first Jaico Impression: 2017

Printed by
SAP Print Solutions Pvt. Ltd.
28 A, Laxmi Industrial Estate, S. N. Path
Lower Parel (W), Mumbai - 400 013

I dedicate this book to the

CHINMAYA MISSION

A spiritual organization, that has been teaching the practical relevance of ancient Indian scriptures in modern times

— Dr Radhakrishnan Pillai

I dedicate this book to

My wife Lalitha and my daughters Archana and Jyotsna

&

My extended family, the Maharashtra Police Force
Consisting of lakhs of police officers, men and women
who dedicate their lives for the safety and security
of the state's citizens

I dedicate my proceeds from this book entirely for the
education of policemen's children

— D Sivanandhan

Notes

- This is a management and leadership book. However, we have kept the writing style simple, so that those without a management or leadership background can also learn from the book.

- This book is a continuation of ideas given in the first book, *Corporate Chanakya*. If you have already read it, you will understand these concepts much better. If not, we suggest you read the first book also to get a better understanding of Chanakya's teachings that can be applied in different situations one comes across.

- The original *sutras* of Chanakya have been used in this book. They are English translations given in *Kautilya's Arthashastra* by RP Kangle from the University of Mumbai, Sanskrit Department and published by Motilal Banarasidas. Those interested in studying the original *Arthashastra* fully are advised to read it. Various translations of the *Arthashastra* by other scholars are also available in the market.

- This is a book with practical application. Therefore, pages have been given for you to make your personal notes. Do apply the learning in your workplaces and personal lives. We will be happy to know your success story. Do write to us at *info@ciplmumbai.in*

- If you have loved the concepts of Chanakya, make sure you teach the same to others. Begin as a student of Chanakya, but aim to be a teacher of Chanakya's wisdom.

- Spreading knowledge only increases your own knowledge.

Trust me, it has worked for me and it will work for you as well....

Acknowledgements

USUALLY, AFTER WRITING a first book that goes on to become a bestseller, many think it is easy to write the second book. It is far from the truth in my case.

This book took more time and energy than the first book. More than 200 meetings were held over two years between myself, Sivanandhan sir and the Jaico team. A lot of time was spent in research to understand the working of the police system; studying various books, websites and magazines; collecting data; meeting and interviewing various people who worked with Sivanandhan sir.

With my busy travel schedule and research and teaching commitments at the University, it was impossible to do everything myself. I asked the Jaico team to give me editorial support in this project, which was becoming bigger by the day. By the time we completed the project, we had so much data and information that the challenge was what 'not' to publish, rather than what to.

I would first like to thank Sivanandhan sir for agreeing to be a part of this book project. He has had several offers, both during his tenure and after his retirement from the police force, to write a book on his experiences. I guess we were lucky to have him agree to this project.

The information that he provided was very valuable. All the facts and figures included in the book give insights into the unique police leadership style of Sivanandhan sir. Sivanandhan sir and I spent time in our homes, restaurants, offices, hotels, in flights, airports and even in the university to check and recheck each detail we had gathered during the research for this book. This was a massive exercise by itself.

Jaico Publishing House – Akash Shah, Ashwin Shah and Mr Sharma are my guides in the publishing world. They spotted me as a talent and made a bestselling author out of me. The editorial team including Sandhya, Lakshmi, Poornima and Pragya, who supported me at every stage, were more like a family that helped this book reach the final destination of publication. They have been very patient and committed throughout. Nita, who designed the wonderful cover page for the book deserves special appreciation. The cover is different, yet a continuation of my first book, *Corporate Chanakya*.

The marketing and sales team including Vijay, Steven and all the branch managers and salespersons at Jaico's ten offices across India gave inputs for the betterment of this book.

Chanakya Institute of Public leadership (CIPL) – the team at the University of Mumbai, Department of Philosophy, was always there to encourage me on this project.

Ranjit Shetty, Director at CIPL took my workload while I was focusing on writing this book. My students and now office staff, Malathi Thevar and Viraj Padhariya were my research assistants. I could ask for any reference from the *Arthashastra* and I would get the information in less than a minute. This showed their deep study of the book.

The other professors at the department were always supportive. A special thanks to Dr Meenal Katarnikar, our faculty member at the Kautilya Arthashastra research project, where we run a six-months public leadership course.

I would also like to thank all my students of the *Arthashastra*, who have committed their lives to practicing Chanakya's teachings. They have decided to change the course of our nation. Most of them have joined public life, the political field and other socially relevant careers.

Thank you to my teacher and guides during the study and research and PhD work of the *Arthashastra* – Dr Gangadharan Nair, from Chinmaya International foundation and Dr Shubhada Joshi, Head of the Department of Philosophy, University of Mumbai, because of whom I have been able to take the wisdom of Chanakya into the academic field.

Our Vice-Chancellor, Dr Rajan Welukar who released my first book, *Corporate Chanakya* on 15 August, 2010, and without his continuous support, this second book would not have been possible.

My special thanks to KJ Somaiya Bharatiya Sanskriti Peetham, from where I did my MA in Sanskrit (through Kavikulaguru Kalidas Sanskrit University). My special thanks to Shri Samir Somaiya, Dr Kala Acharya, Dr Lalita Namjoshi and the entire team at Somaiya for guiding me.

Thanks to Dr Chandraprakash Dwivedi, who made *Chanakya* the TV serial, which has inspired many people like me to understand the contribution of Chanakya to India.

Chinmaya Mission – I am a product of Chinmaya Mission. This spiritual organization has given me everything. Without my study of the *Arthashastra* at Chinmaya Mission, neither my first book nor this book would have been possible. Special thanks to Swami Tejomayanandaji, the current global head who encouraged me to study ancient scriptures in the traditional *Gurukul* and *Guru-Shishya Parampara*. I would also like to thank Swami Advayanandaji – the head of Chinmaya International Foundation; Swami Sacchidanandaji, who taught me what management is, as a school going child and the hundreds of spiritual teachers of the Chinmaya Mission across the globe, who have been supporting my mission of spreading the knowledge available in the *Arthashastra*.

My family has always supported me by managing my erratic work and travel schedules. Surekha – I know you are the best mother a child can get. Thanks for taking care of my children

- Aanvikshiki and Arjun - in their most formative years. While I teach leadership and management across the globe, you are teaching them spiritual values, which is the first step towards leadership. A special thanks to my parents CKK Pillai and Sushila K Pillai; parents-in-law - Shekhar and Dhanavati Shetty and sisters-in-law, Sarikha and Chandrika.

MTHR Global - Thank you to my friends from the organization, More than Human Resource (*www.mthrglobal.com*) - from where the name, *Corporate Chanakya* emerged. Rajesh Kamath, Vipul Agarwal, Ashish Gakrey, Rajesh Gupta, Preeti Malhotra and Keyur Jani have been giving a new look to Indian management in the HR industry.

SPM group of companies - Without the support of Muulraj Chheda, Pravin Chheda, Rajen Chheda, Niket and their spouses, I would not have been able to devote all my time to spreading Chanakya's teachings. I am what I am because of the support of the SPM family in the initial days of spreading Chanakya's teachings. I continue to be on the board of the SPM Foundation, which is doing lot of noble work in society.

Thank you to Venkat Iyer, my childhood friend and partner in my spiritual tourism business. Your friendship is more valuable to me than all the riches in the world. Let God give everyone a friend like you, who stands like a solid rock in good and bad times. Pankaj Joshi, Milind Agarwal and Rajesh Ajgaonkar have given me new dimensions of thinking to take Chanakya's teachings forward.

Friends in the police force – Sandeep Karnik, IPS and Satish Menon (Railway Protection Force) were my school friends who joined the police force. It was nice to see friends as cops for the first time in my life. They have always given valuable insights on the workings of a policeman. Both stand today as role models in the police force.

Shemaroo Entertainment – That is another family of mine.

Madhuri and Hiren Gada, Atul Maru and the whole team have been instrumental in taking Chanakya's teachings to the world through various projects like the management film, *Chanakya Speaks*, audio book and training kit.

Friends in the corporate world – A big thank you to Dr Ajit Ranade and Ashish Dwivedi from the Aditya Birla group; Tarang Jain, MD of Varroc group; Sushil Wadhwa, Chairman of Claris Pharmaceuticals; Shashi Kiran Shetty, CMD of Allcargo; Asit Koticha and Sameer Koticha of ASK group; MP Ramachandran, CMD of Jyothy Laboratories and Satish Shenoy from L&T. All of them have taken special efforts to promote Chanakya's teachings within their organizations and in various business circles.

Educational and academic institutions – My sincere thanks to the principals, teachers, professors and directors of various colleges and management schools who were instrumental in inviting me to speak as a guest lecturer. They also suggested my book as reference material on Indian management and encouraged students to do research projects on Chanakya.

The best was the introduction of Chanakya's thoughts in the institutions of the armed forces like the Defence Services Staff College (DSSC), National Defence College (NDC) and Institute of Defence and Strategy Analysis (IDSA). Vice-Admiral Gaikwad, Wing Commander Aditya Kiran, Col Nair, Col Pradeep Gautam and the respective Commanding Officers of these institutions were instrumental in making Chanakya's warfare strategy a matter of serious study in military science.

Author friends – A big thank you to Amish Tripathi, Ashwin Sanghi, Rashmi Bansal, Devdutt Pattanaik, Anita and Harsha Bhogle, Rushabh Turakhia, Santosh Nair, Mukta Mahajani... all of them bestselling authors themselves regularly gave me valuable tips to make the second book better than the first.

Thank you to bookstores including Crossword, Landmark, Sapna, Reliance, Media Mart and various others across India and their teams who recommended the book to their customers; and to various online bookstores which promoted Chanakya and the e-book versions online.

Politicians – My gratitude to Shri Rajesh Tope, Education minister of Maharashtra; Shri Sanjay Dina Patil, Member of Parliament; Shri Prithviraj Chauhan, Chief Minister of Maharashtra and Shri Narendra Modi, Chief Minister of Gujarat who have encouraged other politicians and government officials to study *Corporate Chanakya* and apply the teachings in their respective *workplaces*.

And finally, thank you to the millions of Chanakya fans like you, who not just read my book but also gifted it to others. Chanakya and management would not have been famous and relevant in our generation without your support.

Dr Radhakrishnan Pillai,
Mumbai

Contents

Preface

SOME PEOPLE GET lucky. And some get very lucky.

But people like me call it the Grace of God or *Guru Kripa*.

My first book, *Corporate Chanakya* published by Jaico turned out to be a bestseller. It broke many records in sales in the field of management books. It was in the bestseller list ever since its release. It got translated into ten regional languages – Hindi, Marathi, Gujarati, Assamese, Oriya, Bengali, Tamil, Malayalam, Telugu and Kannada.

It was brought out as an audio book, again turning out to be a bestseller in the audio book category. The book inspired the world's first management film based on Chanakya's teachings, *Chanakya Speaks* (*www.chanakyaspeaks.in*). Within a month of its release, the film received the Award of Merit at the Indie Fest (Calfornia).

Owing to the success of the book, I was invited to speak and lecture in over hundred institutes, colleges and universities across ten countries in less than two years. It also helped me set up our institute, Chanakya Institute of Public Leadership (*www.ciplmumbai.in*) in the Department of Philosophy at the University of Mumbai. It is the first institute of its kind in the world, which teaches the *Arthashastra*.

The journey has just begun and there is a lot to be done in years to come. I feel the hand of God behind all this success.

Success brings problems with it. Can I repeat this success? The first book set a benchmark, and ever since its release people have been asking me, "When is your next book coming?"

For me the question was different.....

Instead of 'when' my next book would come the question was, 'what' will my next book be about.

I struggled with this question for many days and months, which rolled into years. I knew clearly that the subject would be Chanakya, yet I did not want to write *Corporate Chanakya* – part 2. The first book was complete in itself, yet continuity was needed for my old readers.

Chanakya was a man of action. What he said was not just theory, but what could be practiced and applied. What worked in the past can work in the present too. I wanted to bring back Chanakya in our generation.

How I would deal with such a great legend in my next book was a question that I was deliberating on for a long time. I knew all the theories of leadership given in the *Arthashastra*. Yet, there are chances of them just being theories, without any practical value to you and me.

I got my answer the day I met D Sivanandhan....

He was the Director-General of Maharashtra Police at that time, a few months away from retirement from the topmost police rank. I had heard about him and the work he had done. We were sharing a dais for a leadership program for ophthalmology doctors. That day, I spoke on the theory of leadership and Sivanandhan sir spoke on the 'practical' aspects of leadership. He spoke about situational leadership, transformational leadership and what goes into the making of a leader!

As I was listening, a quiet bell rang in my mind. "Here stands a man of action. He has delivered against all odds. I talk about it, whereas he has done it!"

For me, Sivanandhan sir became a person who was a real-life leader, who had practiced all that Chanakya had said.

The next week I met Sivanandhan sir in his office with my students from Mumbai University. We were supposed to be with him for half an hour but in spite of his busy schedule, he gave us two-and-a-half hours. The students could ask him any questions and he gave them quick and detailed answers. I came to know that before joining the police force, he was also a professor of economics. The teacher in me – met the teacher in him.

From there, a relationship developed, where we kept meeting each other again and again. I knew he was someone whom the police force, the government and our nation was proud of.

He was a man of achievement, yet there were many aspects about him that very few people knew. He was always in the limelight, yet very few had seen the complete picture of his life. Many more meetings followed and I came to know him well. There were wonderful incidents and stories that he narrated, which many did not know about.

And then, a meeting between Sivanandhan sir and my publishers, Jaico finally brought clarity to the book you are holding.

The theme of this book is surely on Chanakya; yet it is different from the first. I have written on leadership, but taking Sivanandhan sir as a case study, as an example of great and transformational leadership.

In this book, you will find a leadership model of Chanakya. You will also find that leadership model being brought alive by Sivanandhan and what he did during his days in the police force as a leader. He set high standards for others, becoming a role model.

This book is about theory meeting practice, leadership concepts meeting application, age old formulae meeting modern-day success stories.

Chanakya's leadership ideas, comes alive with Sivanandhan sir.

Introduction

Chanakya's 7 Secrets
of Strategic Leadership

Leadership – the Concept

IN THE ARTHASHASTRA, Chanakya refers to the leader as *Vijigishu*, meaning one who wants to be victorious and conquer in spite of the challenges. Even today, a leader has to think like a conqueror and succeed, irrespective of the circumstances.

Leadership as a concept has been evolving over the centuries. "Leader" initially referred to the king of a country or nation. Today, we have leaders in every field – politics, business, science, academics, administration, armed forces, society, community, various unions, sports teams and even spirituality. Some leaders may have a large following; others may not. Some leaders are great orators and public speakers, while others sit quietly at their desks or laboratories and become "thought leaders". They give a new direction and perspective to the way people think.

Some leaders are immensely popular when they are alive; their work attains speed and recognition in that generation. Other leaders are celebrated after they are dead, because they were much ahead of their times and their generation could not understand their greatness. Some leaders, such as Lokmanya Tilak, Rabindranath Tagore or Thiruvalluvar are known in their particular regions, in a village, a community or a nation. Others like Mahatma Gandhi, Napoleon, Albert Einstein or Abraham Lincoln gain worldwide recognition.

Yet, all these leaders have something in common, some factors that earned them respect and appreciation, which we also call attributes of leadership.

So what exactly is leadership?

Across the globe, leadership has become a subject of serious discussion, study and research. Universities now have centers of leadership. The number of books written on leadership has been growing rapidly.

In India, leadership has been taken very seriously. Today, all eyes are on India, as it is among the fastest growing economies of the world. India is new, yet old. A young nation which got independence in 1947 has a history, culture and tradition of over 10,000 years. As in any other nation, India and Indians draw inspiration from the heroes and leaders of the past. As a country of over a billion people, we are proud of the achievements of our past leaders. Our leaders such as Gandhi and Emperor Ashoka inspired and created more leaders across the globe. Others like Shivaji, Subhash Chandra Bose, Sardar Patel, Jawaharlal Nehru, Rajendra Prasad, Lal Bahadur Shastri and other freedom fighters inspire our present generation and inject patriotism in the youth.

When we go back further in time, we find leadership lessons from superheroes like Krishna, Rama and Buddha in epics like the *Ramayana* and *Mahabharata*. For Indians, these lessons are part of their thinking, a part of daily living and discussions.

However, a unique factor about India is that we also learn from the person who created the leader, the "leadership guru". The leader is important, but the creator of the leader is more important, because a leadership guru can create more leaders. Swami Ramdas guided Shivaji to become a successful king. Ramakrishna inspired Vivekananda to become a giant spiritual leader.

Some people like to study leaders; people like us love to study leadership gurus. And among the leadership gurus, one person stands out as the epitome of leadership teachings - Chanakya.

Chanakya was the guru of Chandragupta Maurya, the first king of the Maurya dynasty and the grandfather of Emperor Ashoka who spread the golden teachings of Buddhism across the globe. Chanakya has been credited by many historical scholars as the first person in world history to create the concept of a nation or *rashtra*. Aspects of his teachings have been documented in his work *The Kautilya Arthashastra*, written in the 4th century BC

Over the last several years, I have been a student and teacher of the *Arthashastra*. Having learnt the *Arthashastra* under Dr Gangadharan Nair at the Chinmaya International Foundation (*www.chinfo.org*), I have discovered many ancient Indian models of leadership. I am amazed how Chanakya's leadership models are relevant even today. They are not just ancient; they are eternal.

One of the leadership models given in the *Arthashastra* is "Chanakya's Saptangah" — the seven pillars of a kingdom. These pillars of old, forgotten over the years, can be interpreted as the "seven secrets of leadership" in the modern-day context. A training module on this was developed and we have been conducting leadership development programs across the globe.

We have trained leaders in corporations and business groups, in the armed forces and the police, as well as scientists, academicians, social organizations, spiritual institutions, government departments and many others.

It was inspiring to see that this leadership model was relevant to all the sectors of society, in India and abroad.

Chanakya's Seven Pillars of Leadership

Chanakya describes this leadership model in Book 6, Chapter 1, Verse 1 of the *Arthashastra*.

"Swami, Amatya, Janpada, Durg, Kosha, Dand,
Mitra iti Prakritya" (6.1.1)

(The king, the minister, the country, the fortified city, the treasury, the army and the ally are the constituent elements of the state.)

Any kingdom can be classified into seven parts, which put together make the kingdom complete.

▲ Chanakya's 7 Secrets of Leadership		
The Secret	Represents	Today in an organization
▲ 1 Swami	The king (The leader)	The leader
▲ 2 Amatya	The minister (The king's advisors and councilors, manager)	The manager
▲ 3 Janpada	The country (The citizens)	Marketing/ Customers

▲ 4	Durg	The fort (The housing)	Infrastructure
▲ 5	Kosha	The treasury (Money)	Finance
▲ 6	Dand	The Army (The team)	Teamwork
▲ 7	Mitra	The Ally (The friend)	Consultants/ Mentors

A happy kingdom consists of an ideal king (*swami*) as a leader, guided by able ministers (*amatya*), who takes care of the citizens (*janpada*), providing them good infrastructure and facilities (*durg*), making sure the treasury (*kosha*) of the state and the people is always full, which is protected by an able army (*dand*) and helped by good allies (*mitra*).

This model gives us a big picture of leadership. Leaders need to look at the forest, whereas most of us usually look at only the trees.

In a company, a person working in the IT department will focus on issues connected to his area of work. The accounts department only looks at financial numbers. The marketing and sales team will focus only on customers and clients. The production department is concerned about the number of units manufactured. This is looking at the company in parts.

A chairman or CEO will need to understand all these departments separately and in a unified manner. The chairman knows that the work of each department is separate and unique, but that they are interdependent. To look at the big and the small simultaneously is a leader's skill.

Can the finance person understand marketing and production? Can the marketing person understand what the human resource (HR) department does? Can the HR department go beyond recruitment and administrative work? This is looking at the big picture. This is a leadership approach.

There is often a misconception that if a person in the production department starts to learn about the functioning of other departments, he may become less productive in his own work. However, the reverse is true. The production person will improve his skill set and become a more productive employee. An HR person who understands the functions and roles of other departments becomes a better HR person.

Then why do most of us look at only the parts and not the whole? This is due to our past training and background. Our families, education and environment are responsible for the way we think. So, if you are a chartered accountant, you have been trained in dealing with financial numbers and reports. An HR person is educated and trained to handle IR (industrial relations), salaries, interviews, manpower planning and issues connected with his particular area of work. Over a period of time, you become a specialist in your area. Today, it is called an era of "super specialization".

There is nothing wrong in being a specialist. But in the process, we miss the big picture. We forget to look at the company and only look at the department. The point is – do not limit yourself to a particular department; consider the big picture. Think like a chairman or CEO; this is the leadership way of looking at the company.

Today, courses such as "Finance for Non-Finance Managers" are becoming quite popular. Such courses teach you to look at the same company from a different perspective. They train you to think holistically and not piecemeal. This is leadership training. Good companies train their employees across departments and functions. In turn, they make the employees great leaders.

Chanakya's Seven Pillars of Leadership model also trains one to look at both the forest and the trees. The trees without the forest and the forest without the trees are both incomplete. But knowing that both are interdependent makes us more aware of our environment and the conditions in which we operate.

This book explains the Seven Pillars of Leadership model and uses it to teach you about leadership. We call it the seven secrets of leadership. In this book, we have shown you how the model is being applied in the Indian policing system. However, the model is not just about police leadership; the principles of this model can be applied to leadership in any arena.

In this book, you will see both the theory and practice of leadership, Chanakya in thought and action. You will see ancient India and present India together. This book has an interdisciplinary approach. We have connected Chanakya's leadership theories and application in D. Sivanandhan's police leadership. More important, the book will help you to discover the leader in you.

You may be a businessman, policeman, dean of an educational institution, a homemaker or a student entering the job market. Each person can learn about leadership. A person who is not a leader can become a leader by applying these seven secrets. An existing leader can become a better leader by following these principles. If you are a parent, you can teach these principles to your children and make them leaders of the future. Each chapter in the book provides tips to apply these principles in your personal and professional life.

Read on to understand leadership. Read on to become a leader.

Leadership in the Police Force

The leader has to be clear about his goals, objectives and responsibilities, because he has to give direction to his team. The highest form of leadership is transformational leadership, where one transforms the organizational culture to a positive, productive and result-oriented culture. For instance, the Green Revolution or the telecom revolution transformed India. Every person in the nation reaped the benefits of these revolutions. Transformational leadership has similar results.

It is often questioned whether one person alone can transform the whole system. In reality, only one person can transform and create change. Of course, team effort makes the change possible. Yet, the whole process of change begins with that one person who created the change — the transformational leader.

Different types of leaders require different skill sets, because the objective of each leader is different. In political leadership, the vision of the person with a missionary zeal is important. Chief ministers like Narendra Modi and Nitish Kumar are political leaders who have made the states of Gujarat and Bihar among the most developing states of India. The government of any state has the required resources, both human and physical, as well as an administrative system at its command. Once the political will for change gets fired up, the system gears for positive action and changes take place almost immediately.

In corporate leadership, once resources like money are available through various funding agencies or IPOs, the organization can get into action and create products or services. It can employ the best brains, set timelines and launch products. Steve Jobs, as a corporate leader, successfully launched the iPhone, iPod and iPad within a short period of time. Ratan Tata launched the Nano at the price he wanted to offer to customers.

Is leadership in policing any different? For that, one needs to understand that the objective of police in India is maintenance of law and order and crime prevention and control.

However, within the ambit of these broad objectives lie various unknowns. Anything and everything out of the ordinary seems to require policing — riot control, traffic control, maintenance of communal harmony, protection of a VIP and a common man, investigation of crime, handling Naxalism, tackling terrorism — the list is endless. We cannot define the role of the police as easily as we can define a company's role, where the results can be easily measured by sales targets.

Moreover, one mistake in the police is a matter of life and death. New types of crime emerge every so often. For example, cyber crime was unheard of 20 years ago, but is a big part of police investigations today.

Policing is a very dynamic activity. It is round-the-clock work. Therefore, police leadership requires many more skills than other types of leadership. On the one hand, the police works on eliminating the underworld don; on the other hand, it also helps a lost child reach home. It is about making women feel secure and senior citizens feel safe at home. It is about stopping a crazy youth from speeding on his motorbike; it is also about allowing an adult boy and girl to exercise their legal right to choose their marriage partner, despite their parents' opposition.

Yet, our society does not give due respect to the role of the police. This is not to say that all policemen are perfect. There is corruption in the system; some policemen are no better than criminals in uniform. However, not all policemen are corrupt or criminals. Policing is an essential part of society, and without it, a society will collapse.

The challenges faced by the police force are unimaginable. When the country celebrates festivals like Diwali, Ganesh Chaturthi, Durga Pooja, Independence Day, Eid or Christmas, the police has no holidays. The duty of a policeman is 24 hours and he has to report to work for 12 hours a day. They have no family lives to speak of. A policeman's wife lives with the worry of her husband becoming the target of a criminal's bullet. It is difficult to find suitable bridegrooms for policemen's daughters. What's more, boys in police uniform are not considered ideal matches for prospective marriages. There are no unions to fight for policepersons' rights; they get much lower salaries than their counterparts in the corporate world. In fact, most senior police officers are intelligent and sharp enough to have been CEOs of multinational companies, had they taken that route. The media is constantly at their heels for breaking news. Policemen also go through tremendous stress due to constant political pressures.

Consider this. Mumbai has a population of around 2 crore, and the number of policemen and policewomen is 42,000. Half of them work in the day and the other half during the night, since they have 12-hour workdays. Thus, approximately 20,000 policepersons protect 2 crore people, which makes it around 1,000 people to be protected by each policeperson. That is similar to one salesperson taking care of 1,000 sales accounts. How would you compare stress in a corporate job and a police job?

Also, a policeman has to deal with anybody and everybody — a film star, an illegal migrant, a lunatic or a drunkard on the street, a young student attempting suicide, traffic accidents, passion-driven crimes, extortion calls. Each policeman constantly deals with the unknown.

The police force is constantly faced with lack of resources and manpower. Yet, their target is to establish peace in society. When they have achieved the target and there is peace, no one thinks about them. When the crime rate is high, they are blamed. The presence of the police is not felt; but their absence is. Because of all these reasons, policing is often called a thankless job.

Yet in the same system and society, what brings hope of a better future is good leadership in the police force. In this whole mess, there emerges a leader who inspires everybody from top to bottom, someone who disciplines them like a father and cares for them like a mother.

This book is about those police officers who have, time and again, infused hope in lakhs of men and women and pride in the uniform they wear. The happiness they get when they look back in their careers and say, "Yes, we took the right decision to join the force," comes from the efforts of such leaders. Such leaders instill a sense of achievement in policemen, making them feel they have contributed to society and helped in nation building.

D Sivanandhan is a case study throughout the book. Yet, this book is about the police force which stood strong with the leader. It is about many other leaders before him who displayed leadership in different forms. This book is written for future police leaders as a document for reference. And for the young men and women who can believe in themselves and say, "I too can be like Sivanandhan and turn the tide." As they say, leadership is to succeed "in spite of", not "because of".

This book is also for a common man like you and me. Next time, when we see a traffic policeman doing his job in the hot afternoon, instead of feeling angry and labeling him corrupt and inefficient, we could empathize with him and say, "Thank you sir, for what you do; I know my wife and children are safe at home..."

Who Was Chanakya?

BORN IN THE 4th Century BC, in India, Chanakya was also known as Vishnugupta and Kautilya. Through centuries, scholars have described Chanakya as a rare mastermind who became an expert in varied and specialized fields like management, economics, politics, law, leadership, governance, warfare, military tactics, strategy, finance, accounting and several others.

He was responsible for bringing down the Nanda dynasty and establishing his able student, Chandragupta Maurya on the throne as the Emperor. He is therefore called the "kingmaker". He is also credited with masterminding the defeat of Alexander in India, who was on his march to conquer the world.

As a political thinker, Chanakya visualized the concept of a "nation" for the first time in human history. During his time, India was split into various kingdoms. He brought them all together under one central governance, thus creating a nation called Aryavartha, which later became India.

He documented his lifelong work in his books, *Kautilya's Arthashastra* and *Chanakya Niti*.

The *Arthashastra* has 6000 sutras, classified into 15 books, 150 chapters and 180 topics by Chanakya himself.

Many philosophical concepts about leadership in the *Arthashastra* like *Aanvikshiki* (the science of thinking), *Rajrishi* (philosopher-king), *Indriyajaya* (one who has control over himself), *Vijigishu* (conqueror) are India's unique contributions to the world.

Scholars and intellectuals across the globe for centuries have been using the *Arthashastra* for guidance on subjects like leadership and governance. For ages, rulers across the world have referred to the *Arthashastra* for building a nation on sound economics, based on spiritual values.

Arthashastra when literally translated means "scripture of wealth" but it contains knowledge about every subject under the sun. It is the knowledge of wealth and a wealth of knowledge.

Chapter 1

Swami

THE LEADER

Swami	the king
Amatya	the minister
Janpada	the country
Durg	the fortified city
Kosha	the treasury
Dand	the army
Mitra	the ally

KAUTILYA'S ARTHASHASTRA IS a book of leadership. It is a guide to and a ready reference for tackling various issues that leaders may face while leading the country. A study of the *Arthashastra* was a must for kings in India for many centuries.

The *Arthashastra* is divided into 15 books. In Book 6, Chanakya defines the seven pillars of the state in the first verse of Chapter 1. He states that the first pillar is the leader himself. An important point must be made here. Even though the *Arthashastra* refers to the leader as "he" (this book will follow the same convention), the qualities of a leader are not restricted to a particular gender. Today, there are women leaders and also leaders from transgender communities. Anyone can become a leader, irrespective of their gender, birthplace and background. So, while reading this book, think, "I too can become a leader."

THE FIRST SECRET

Swami: The Leader

WHO IS A leader? And why does Chanakya place so much emphasis on a leader? Most of us think of a leader as a person with a particular designation and post — the chairman or CEO of a company, the captain of a sports team, the dean of an educational institution or the general of an army. These are leaders no doubt. However, certain other attributes are required to make one a "great leader," a leader who is productive, result-oriented and inspiring.

One may get a leadership chair (position) by heredity, power or influence. But if one is not capable, the chair will not keep you.

— Swami Chinmayananda

What are these attributes and qualities? We will discuss the qualities of a good leader in this chapter.

Before that, let us ask an important question:

▶ **Which would you choose: a good leader or a bad leader?**

The answer is obvious. Everyone aspires to work for the best leaders. However, every organization does not necessarily have good leaders. Therefore, people look for those rare gems who can lead the team to achieve its goals with honesty and efficiency, without resorting to manipulative, unethical or illegal means.

Now let us change the situation and ask the next question:

▶ **Which would you choose: a bad leader or no leader?**

Is this difficult to answer? In most organizations, this is the reality. Everyone wants the leader to be ideal, but the leaders are usually not even close to being perfect. In fact, most of us feel that they are bad leaders, and if they would quit or were replaced, the organization would make great strides towards success.

Imagine that suddenly, such a leader meets with an accident and from the next day onwards, the organization does not have a head. The board continues to look for a replacement. However, an ideal leader is not found for the next one year. As a result, the organization's activities slow down because there is nobody to make strategic decisions and employees are not accountable to anyone. It becomes the story of anybody, then somebody and finally nobody doing the work. Gradually, employees begin thinking that the old leader was not all that bad — at least things were moving, even if slowly. It was better than the organization being directionless and employees feeling like orphans.

This leads us to another important question:

▶ **What if the bad leader becomes a good leader?**

This is possible. And the question we will ask is: how? There are various methods by which a bad leader can become a good leader. Also, many employees can be trained to become leaders. So, if the top leader dies or retires, there is a pool of leaders to choose from, for the top position. This can be achieved by training and developing leadership qualities among all the people in the organization, right from the top to the bottom.

In the army, there is a saying, "A soldier never quits till he is dead." It means if the leader of a group dies during a war, the next one takes up the leadership role and continues the war. If the second person dies, the third person takes over as the leader. There is an inbuilt system in the armed forces that creates leaders in every situation.

One may wonder whether anyone can become a leader. The point here is that in the group that goes to fight the war, everyone is not a General. But even those in the lower ranks have been trained to think like leaders. Leadership is not just by rank or designation; it is by attitude and competence.

In the Mumbai terror attack of November 26, 2008, Tukaram Omble, an assistant police sub-inspector, took a leadership position. He marched ahead, taking bullets on his chest, but caught Ajmal Kasab alive. Omble proved his leadership, irrespective of his designation.

During the same terror attack, the Mumbai police lost 16 men. Of these, only two — Hemant Karkare, Joint Commissioner of Police, Anti Terrorist Squad and Ashok Kamte, Additional Commissioner of Police, Eastern region — were IPS officers. The IPS or Indian Police Service is the highest level of police leadership in India. Both Karkare and Kamte were leaders in the true sense, who had the best training and top positions. The other 14 were police inspectors, sub-inspectors and constables.

Yet all of them proved to be leaders. Today, the country salutes all the 16 men as leaders for their sacrifice, irrespective of their designations. That is "situational leadership" in action. The training and attitude of these men made them come forward and become leaders in a crisis.

We should also note that there were many others who did not die in the operations, but proved their leadership qualities when they took charge and controlled the situation.

Therefore we see that a leader, a *Swami*, according to Chanakya, is a person who takes the initiative and is ready to sacrifice for the higher purpose.

A well-known incident in the life of Dr Abdul Kalam shows how his mentor and leader handled a crisis. Prof Satish Dhawan was then Chairman, Indian Space Research Organization (ISRO) and Dr Kalam was assigned the job to develop the first satellite launch vehicle SLV-3, to put the satellite, Rohini in orbit. This was one of the largest high-technology space programs undertaken in 1973. The entire space technology community, men and women, were geared for this task. The hard work of thousands of scientists, engineers and technicians resulted in the first SLV-3 launch on August 10, 1979.

SLV-3 took off in the early hours and the first stage worked beautifully. Even though all the stage rockets and systems worked, the mission could not achieve its objectives, as the control system malfunctioned in the second stage. Instead of being placed in orbit, the satellite sank in the Bay of Bengal. The mission was a failure.

At a press conference at Sriharikota after the event, where both Prof Dhawan and Dr Kalam were present, Prof Dhawan announced that he took responsibility for not achieving the mission, even though Dr Kalam was the project director and mission director.

Later, when SLV-3 was re-launched on July 18, 1980, successfully putting Rohini into orbit, at the subsequent press conference, Prof Dhawan put Dr Kalam in front to share the success story with the press.

Thus, the leader gives the credit for success to those who worked for it, but absorbs the responsibility for their failure. This incident had a tremendous impact on Dr Kalam's life, and later, he became one of the most respected leaders of India.

In Book 1, Chapter 19, Verses 1–5 of the *Arthashastra*, Chanakya says:

"If the king is energetic, his subjects will be equally energetic. If he is slack (and lazy in performing his duties) the subjects will also be lazy, and thereby, eat into his wealth. Besides, a lazy king will easily fall into the hands of the enemies. Therefore, the king should himself always be energetic."

Leaders set an example and become role models. Even in the *Bhagawad Gita*, Krishna says, "As the leader, so the people."

Therefore, being energetic is very important. A leader must be physically energetic and mentally alert and vigilant.

If the leader is lazy, so will be the followers. The most productive people will become lazy under bad leadership. On the other hand, an energetic and active leader will inspire even lazy people to perform beyond their own expectations.

Chanakya also points out that if the leader is not vigilant and alert, the people will eat into his wealth. So, alertness has a direct impact on the finances of an organization. People who are corrupt are in constant fear of getting caught by the leader. If the leader is not alert, he will invite corruption into the system.

It is most important for the *leader to be energetic*. This means that a leader cannot expect others to motivate him. He should be self-motivated. The difference between motivation and inspiration is that motivation is always "because of," while inspiration is "in spite of." Inspiration for a higher cause, a higher ideal for which he is ready to sacrifice everything is what motivates a leader.

In the police force, the inspiration is the nation. It is an ideal so high, that each policeman is ready to give the ultimate sacrifice of life for it. However, the leader must be the role model here as well. As the saying goes, "When the going gets tough, the tough get going." That is initiative. That is leadership. That is inspiration.

ACCORDING TO CHANAKYA

Leadership Qualities

IN BOOK 6 of the *Arthashastra*, Chanakya describes various qualities of a leader. In this book, we will focus on the key aspects of leadership qualities for a *swami*. These qualities are not a birthright; they must be developed by hard work and consistent efforts.

These qualities are universal principles of leadership. So, if you want to become a leader, practice these qualities. Or, you may observe an ideal leader, they possess these qualities.

The qualities of a *Swami* (Leader) are (Book 6, Chapter 1, Verse 3 of the *Arthashastra*):

▶ Intelligent and dynamic

▶ Associates with elders

▶ Truthful in speech

▶ Does not break promises

▶ Grateful

▶ Desirous of training

▶ Easily approachable

Let us look at each of these in detail.

▶ Intelligent and dynamic

Intelligence and dynamism are two sides of the same coin. Every leader has to be intelligent. Intelligence is often thought to be about academic brilliance or high IQ scores. Research has proved that every person has equal intelligence at birth. However, as time goes by, depending on a person's education and environment, his or her intelligence is sharpened.

One can become more intelligent by making an effort to stretch your mind and intellect. For instance, we see students who put extra efforts and score good marks in exams. Yet, education must remain a continuous and lifelong process. Reading good books, newspapers and research journals will help in making you more aware and informed about the world. But also note that gathering information does not make you intelligent. You need to develop the skill of analyzing the information you have gathered, taking important decisions and acting on those decisions.

If a leader has understood the key problem through his study, research, discussion and analysis, and reached a solution for the problem, that is only the starting point.

The next step is to implement his findings. That is the real challenge where leaders play the key role.

Therefore, the second aspect is being dynamic. It requires initiative, guts and self-confidence to implement your plan. "Plan out your work, and work out your plan," says Swami Chinmayananda. A leader has to do that to prove his leadership abilities.

Implementing a plan is not easy, because there will be many hurdles along the way. Some people never start, thinking of the obstacles they will face. Others start, but stop when they face obstacles. Great leaders start and make sure they succeed, in spite of the problems.

Leaders know what results are and achieve them.

▶ Associates with elders

The Sanskrit word for this is *Vriddhasanyoga*, that is, being in association with elders.

This means learning from "real-life" experts in fields such as leadership, management and finance. Your journey to meet and learn from real-life experts should go on forever.

There are three types of people: those who learn from their mistakes; those who never learn from their mistakes; while the best are those who learn from others' mistakes. "Association with elders" means learning from those who are more mature and experienced than you are.

To keep learning is a great quality of a leader.

▶ Truthful in speech

Speaking the truth is important for a leader. But one step before that is to "understand the truth". This is the key to success. A leader has to find out the truth before taking any decision.

For example, if there is a conflict in an organization, a leader cannot take a hasty decision. He has to talk to people and gather information and evidence. After that, he has to verify and cross-verify the information. If he has found out the truth, the next step is to make sure he accepts the truth and takes a call based on the findings.

Finally, when the leader speaks with regard to the action and decision taken, this is the time to be "truthful in speech". The leader should say what he feels is right and correct. A great leader is one who calls a spade a spade.

A leader needs to face reality and the truth is sometimes bitter. But to stand by the side of truth is leadership. Another great challenge in facing the truth is emotions. A leader needs to remember that "one needs to understand emotions but not get emotional."

In human beings, nature has placed the head above the heart. A leader should let the head rule the heart, and not the other way around.

The "gut" feel most of us talk about in leadership is a mix of head and heart. It is the highest level of leadership when one operates from being intuitive. Many people call intuition the sixth sense. Intuition comes from insights. Insights come from experience and maturity. And maturity comes from understanding the truth.

All great leaders had the quality to understand, face and speak the truth. Most people believe that truth and integrity are good theories, but cannot be practiced in the world today. However, the fact is that only men of truth and integrity prove to be real leaders in the long run. In the end, truth alone triumphs; "*Satyameva Jayate*" says our national symbol (derived from the Mundaka Upanishad).

A leader is truth itself.

▶ **Does not break promises**

Lord Rama in the Indian tradition is regarded as the ideal king. Gandhiji, the father of our nation, promoted the concept of "*Ram-Rajya*", the ideal kingdom of good governance.

In the Tulsi *Ramayana*, there is a famous couplet which talks about the tradition of leadership in Rama's dynasty: "*Raghukul reet sada chali aayi, pran jaaye par vachan na jaayi.*" (The tradition of the Raghu dynasty is that even if we need to sacrifice our lives, we will not break our promises.)

Leadership is not about over-promising and under-delivering. It is about delivering what is promised.

"Walk the talk" is the mantra. It is a very simple, yet profound formula. There are times when even the team does not trust the leader to honor the commitments he makes. That is where leadership emerges. As Narayana Murthy, said in the film,

Chanakya Speaks, "Leadership is making people walk on water... It is making them ready for sacrifice...."

At times, you have to walk alone. Nobel prize winner Rabindranath Tagore wrote in *Geetanjali*, "When the world stops... the leader starts walking...walk alone..."

Remember, it was not the promise that you made to others that you have to keep, but the oath you took when you started on the journey.

In the police force, every recruit takes the "constitutional pledge" to enforce the law of the land when he dons the uniform. So finally, it is about not breaking the promise made to oneself.

That is a leadership promise.

▶ Grateful

Gratefulness means humility. True strength lies in humility. There is a belief that humble people are powerless. But the opposite is true — powerful people are humble.

Let us see humility in action here. Sivanandhan, in his long and illustrious career in the police force, has worked with various seniors, colleagues, subordinates and team members, and dealt with lakhs of people in his various postings. It is not possible for him to remember the names of so many people, but most people would remember him, given that he worked at senior positions.

It happened often that someone he had worked with in the past met him and asked, "Sivanandhan sir, do you remember me? I am so and so and I worked with you at the Thane posting." To avoid the embarrassing situation of saying "No, who are you?" or "What is your name?" Sivanandhan began treating everyone with respect and saying, "Yes sir, how are you?" or "Yes madam, thank you for your good words," even though such persons may have been junior in rank to him. People remembered him for his humility.

You can also try the same when you work as a leader. Thinking "I know all" is a dangerous attitude for a leader.

Giving credit to team members is important. If they perform well, do not take away the limelight. Instead, take a backseat and let the world know who the true hero is. Appreciating someone will only add to your value.

How do you know if you are truly humble? A rich man once went to his guru and said, "I want to develop humility." The guru suggested that he help someone who is lower than him. He did that and came back to the guru and said, "I have helped a poor man today with wealth. Am I humble now?" The guru said, "No," and asked him to help another man lower than him. But after repeated visits to different people, he finally asked his guru, "When will I become humble?" The wise old man replied, "You will have obtained humility when you can no longer find anyone that you think is lower than you in any way!"

Everyone may not be equal in power, status or wealth. But the day you realize that everyone is equal in the eyes of God...

...The leader in you is born.

▶ Desirous of training

Being desirous of training has two aspects: the desire to get trained and training others. These are two sides of the same coin. Training is a very important part of our lives. When we are born into this world, we are completely dependent on our parents and the environment. They slowly train us in walking, talking, toilet manners and dealing with the external world.

When we go to school, we are taught to read, write, socialize and become competent in many other skills. As we grow up, we take professional courses to build competencies that will make us employable. Till this stage of life, we are in a high learning mode. But once we are settled in our lives with a profession or job, we become complacent.

This is dangerous. From here, one has to develop the attitude of continuous learning. Keep learning and push yourself for more knowledge in your respective field. It is said that the secret of success is not just to learn, but to unlearn, relearn and continuously learn.

Leaders know this. They learn from books and also from people; from reports, newspapers and data provided by government agencies. It becomes their passion to keep learning. They are never full; they keep opening themselves to new possibilities.

Learning should stop only when you die. Buddha was on his deathbed and visitors flocked to meet him. A disciple asked, "Why do you meet so many people in this stage?" He said, "So that I can learn a little more from each person before I go."

One has to learn regularly and continuously. This is being desirous of training. But one who is trained should also train others. Never keep your knowledge to yourself. It has to be shared with others. A true leader never worries about knowledge being stolen or taken away by others. In fact, knowledge grows when it is shared. When a candle is used to light another candle, its flame does not reduce. Every candle should ignite fire in many other candles. That is the true fulfillment of life.

A leader ensures that training of the highest quality is given to the team members. Whether people stay with you for the long-term, short-term or medium-term, investment in training has to be of the highest standards. Great leaders build good training systems and institutions. They are involved in the training themselves. They design the programs and also make sure the best people are invited to share their knowledge and wisdom.

This is fulfillment of leadership.

▶ Easily approachable

A leader makes himself available to the people when they require him, not just when he requires them.

The leader plays multiple roles at the same time. He is father and mother, friend, philosopher and guide. A leader is like a ready and available resource for any problem within the organization. People do not just look upon the leader. They look upon him with hope. And having a leader who takes care of his people is a great blessing.

As a leader in the police, Sivanandhan knew the problems of the system. Obedience is expected at the highest level in the police from your subordinates. A person should be ready to die if his leader gives that order. But Sivanandhan knew that he had to take care of his subordinates as well. To take care of them, he needed to know their thoughts, sentiments and behavior.

Giving unrestricted entrance to people is important. A problem can be handled well if it is in a nascent stage. If decisions are not taken then, it becomes uncontrollable. For the information and data to come to you at the initial stages itself, an open-door policy or being easily approachable is required.

In the olden days too, the kings had a *Janta Durbar*, a place where the king used to meet the common man. The word "king" may not be relevant today, but each one of us is a king in his or her world. Whichever post you hold at the top, middle or bottom, you are the king of your world and the people below you look to you for guidance and decisions.

So create your own *Janta Durbar* and let information flow to you like iron filings move towards a magnet. Be a problem solver and quick decision maker.

The leader in you is now helping others in the true sense.

Practicing the leadership qualities

All these qualities are interconnected and signify the various dimensions of a leader. You may wonder where to start from — which quality to develop first. In a circle, every point is a starting point as well as an ending point.

Start by practicing any of these qualities. You will be surprised that the remaining qualities will slowly develop on their own. For example, if you start reading more, you will become more informed and intelligent. At the same time, because you become aware of other possibilities, you will naturally start looking at things differently and become humble in attitude. Or, if you want to practice being grateful, start with an open-door policy. Respect every person who comes to meet you.

Leadership is being equal to all. Each of you can also develop this by treating your servants, drivers or subordinates with respect.

Take any of these qualities of leadership and start practicing. The important part is to start "practicing". Knowing the qualities and theories of leadership is not enough. To become a leader, one has to think like a leader; to think like a leader, one has to act like a leader. And to act like a leader, it has to come from the heart.

Let the leader in each one of you awaken.

PART C

LEADERSHIP IN ACTION

Tackling Organized Crime

You cannot choose your battlefield, the Gods do that for you;
But you can plant a standard, where a standard never flew.

NATHALIA CRANE

IN THE 1990s, the situation in Mumbai was not just bad, but very bad. Fear psychosis had taken over and gangsters from the underworld ruled the city.

The first duty of any government is to provide security to its people. Security does not mean having hundred guards protecting you. It is a feeling of being safe. If that feeling is not ensured and everyone is worried about their very survival, it is living death. People in Mumbai had lost the feeling of security.

It was October 1997. A gangster, Javed Fawda, was killed in a police operation. A PIL was filed against the Mumbai police, alleging that it was an illegal killing. When Judge AS Aguiar was asked to enquire into the matter, he not only looked into that incident, but also found 95 other questionable matters of police action against gangsters. This included the killings of Sada Pawle and Vijay Tandel in police operations.

As a result, the police force was demoralized. After that, the police avoided taking any strong action against organized crime. The same police operation specialists who had become larger than life at that time were now on the defensive, because they were accused of false police operation killings of Pawle, Tandel and various other gangsters. This gave a boost to the organized crime syndicate and shooting and violence continued unabated.

The underworld took the city to ransom. In 1998 alone, in 93 incidents, 101 people were killed by the underworld. The police became mere spectators and the law and order situation became a leadership failure, to the extent that no marriages were taking place, no cars were purchased, no flats were sold and no high-profile dinners were organized, because of fear of extortion. If you had a fancy car, gangsters demanded money; if you arranged a marriage, they demanded money. In the financial capital of the country, capital was not flowing in; instead, it was flowing out.

Imagine a situation from October 1997 through July 1, 1998, where the police had not taken any strong action.

What was desperately required in this situation was just one thing: police leadership.

In these tense times, Sivanandhan was brought from the jungles of Gadchiroli on July 1, 1998 to Mumbai as Joint Commissioner of Police, Crime (Jt. CP, Crime). He was the only addition to the Mumbai police force of that time.

He had six months of that year left to perform. He had the whole-hearted support of RH Mendonca, then Commissioner of Police, Mumbai city. In addition, he also had the trust and backing of the entire force. And in retrospect, he would credit the success of his achievements to the entire team.

This was also the time when India moved from a country with just one national channel for years to more than a hundred television channels.

The real-time news channels were a blessing and a curse at the same time for the police, like a two-edged sword. The information subordinates would give to Sivanandhan previously, would be flashed all over the country, even before someone in the police department could know. Thus, the news channels became informers even to the policemen. If the police force managed the information well, they could take advantage. If they failed, there would be public outcry and even the government's stability could be endangered.

One day, Sivanandhan was watching a housewife's interview on a television news channel. She said, "I am afraid that my husband, who goes out in the morning, will not come back in the evening. Until he reaches, I am not sure if he is alive and will ever come back." This statement was like an electric shock for Sivanandhan.

As a police officer who had taken the oath to protect citizens, he thought, "This is not the way citizens should feel. We should be able to give them protection. If this housewife is not feeling safe, I am not doing my job."

The leader in him had awakened.

It was time for action.

But what was the action plan?

The first thing to do was to boost the morale of the police force.

He called his men and told them, "The pending enquiry commission court matter is taking its own time. But we will give you all the legal assistance. So, leave the past behind and let us perform in the present situation."

The next step was to give the policepersons legal protection. He met VR Manohar, a famous lawyer, and apprised him of the facts. Manohar defended the police and eventually got them a very favorable judgment from the Bombay High Court in February, 1999.

However, the challenge was, before the Bombay High Court judgment came, the police had to be motivated. The time for action was now; the police could not afford to waste time in waiting for the court's judgment. The fear that had paralyzed the police system was: what if they took action and the High Court punished the police itself? Sivanandhan had to lead from the front to get the system moving.

He called his team and motivated them by saying, "You take strong action against organized crime, and I will look after you." This, however, did not ensure legal protection. He continued, "My name can be in the FIR. You can make me an accused in case the High Court decides to hang people who have taken action."

But motivational lectures and great promises are not enough in leadership.

He had to back up the team with the resources they required. And among the first resources was money. In a country like ours, at a time when the basic necessities like food, clothing and shelter are still problems, how can a person be motivated by just false promises and hope?

Most of the constables live in slums and poor housing conditions, apart from facing various other problems. How they were looked after is a matter which will be discussed in the following chapters. But in this case, the reality was that money did play an important part in the gang wars and the police was used in these gang wars.

The common practice at that time, it was rumored, was that the police used to take money from the gangs themselves, to eliminate and neutralize one gang against the other. In a way, the gangs were funding the operations. This was absolutely illegal, but the police leaders had no moral control over their own policemen.

As a leader, one should understand the value of money and respect the need for it. Your team members are also human beings and many have large families to feed, educate and take care of. Corruption that comes from "greed" is totally unacceptable. But if a person is corrupt due to basic "need", it is the responsibility of the leader to understand this reality.

Therefore, taking this into account, Sivanandhan made a proposal to the government and got ₹ 1 crore sanctioned as special funds for the operations.

Once the money was allocated, he called in his team – all the constables and inspectors in the 12 teams spread over 12 zones. He then openly distributed it. This was legally acceptable money and they signed receipts for accepting it. Now, there was transparency in dealing. By doing this, he empowered his team multifold. They could buy mobile phones, move all over the country, give informants the necessary incentives. Overall, such empowerment resulted in fantastic operations.

Sivanandhan was one of the officers instrumental in bringing in the MCOCA (Maharashtra Control of Organized Crime Act, 1999) to combat organized crime and terrorism. The preamble to the MCOCA says, "The existing legal framework, i.e. the penal and procedural laws and the adjudicatory system, are found to be rather inadequate to curb or control the menace of organized crime. Government has, therefore, decided to enact a special law with stringent and deterrent provisions including in certain circumstances power to intercept wire, electronic or oral communication to control the menace of organized crime."

Unlike in other laws, under MCOCA, confessions before senior police officers are admissible, not only against the accused giving the confession but also against the other accused in the same case. The accused can also refused anticipatory bail.

The first crime registered under the MCOCA was the attempt to murder Shri Milind Vaidya, the ex-Mayor of Mumbai city. Three others were killed in this attempt. The trial was successfully completed within a year. Three criminals were sentenced to death; seven others got life imprisonment and a collective fine of ₹ 1 crore and 5 lakh.

This quick trial and enhanced punishment sent shivers down the spine of the organized crime sector.

Many subsequent arrests and convictions of high-profile film producers and highly placed people sent the right signal to the criminals, warning them to not take the police for granted.

The police force had been given money, resources and legal help and protection from the High Court, from the judgment, from the press. Training was provided along with strong backing.

The next step was to get the right people. Various capable officers were brought into the team. One such was the Assistant Commissioner of Police (ACP), Dashrath Avhad.

Sivanandhan also encouraged them to become confident and start taking action.

An open challenge was thrown to the team and they took it.

He said, "Together, now let us turn the tide."

On November 11, 1998, the tide turned.

Crime Branch officers had information that some gangsters would kill a targeted person in front of the Arthur Road jail.

The team waited patiently for the gangsters to arrive. When the gangsters, a group of five people, came to the spot, they were surprised to see the police. They started running and were chased up to Dadar. The police opened fire in self-defense and four criminals were shot dead. This operation was the path breaker. Otherwise, until then, it was people who were being killed and the police was on the defensive.

This operation gave the badly required boost to the police morale. The confidence that the police could do better was regained. And then onwards, there was no looking back.

This was followed by many convictions under MPDAA (Maharashtra Prevention of Dangerous Activities Act). Almost 1,500 gangsters and extortionists were detained, 1,500 weapons were recovered and about 300 gangsters were neutralized in police operations. All through this, Sivanandhan had to be continuously alert and show real leadership. Having started it all, they had to win the game.

▶ **Resourceful thinking and strategic information gathering**

Out-of-the-box thinking was required at every moment. An instance of strategic information gathering should be mentioned here. At that time, only a few telephones were being tapped for information. But when Sivanandhan stepped in, he thought of a new way.

It struck him that it would be better to strike at the root of the problem than look at the problem at the superficial level.

Instead of tapping the telephones of small, local gangsters, the police force decided to tap the telephones of gang leaders who were hiding in Pakistan and other countries.

He walked into the Videsh Sanchar Nigam Limited (VSNL) office and talked to the operations manager to get those numbers tapped. So that when gangsters from all over the country would call Pakistan to speak to their gang leaders, the police could obtain fantastic electronic intelligence which gave them the competitive advantage.

For example, the police got information about a plan to kill Pahlaj Nehlani, the film director. The police team waited outside Nehlani's house and neutralized the gangsters who were targeting him. Many other high-profile film personalities like Aamir Khan, JP Datta and Mahesh Bhatt were also on the hit list. By obtaining the information on time, the police were able to neutralize the gangsters.

This was truly strategic leadership. The idea of tapping the telephones of the gang leaders hiding in foreign countries, rather than their foot soldiers in India, was a brilliant breakthrough. As a result of this, the lives of hundreds of people were saved, including prominent people from the film industry, political leaders and industrialists.

From that time onwards, no builder has been shot dead. Whereas, earlier in 1995, builders like Om Prakash Kukreja, Vallabh Thakker, Natwarlal Shah, Thakiyudeen Wahid, Managing Director of East West Airlines, Gulshan Kumar, the famous film producer and music industry tycoon, and Sunit Khatau, the mill owner had become the unfortunate victims of the underworld. These high-profile people had been shot in broad daylight, leading to public outcry. The business community had even declared a "black" Diwali, hoisting black flags to show their extreme unhappiness. It was not just the problem of a city any more. The state of Maharashtra and its assembly, and even Delhi, the national capital, were shaken. This became international news and a cause of deep concern for the economic and security foundations of India.

Therefore, the success of this operation can be gauged from the fact that from 2001 through 2011, until the recent shootout of J Dey, the journalist and Iqbal Kaskar, no shootout had ever taken place.

One hundred and one business people were killed by gangsters in 1998. Sivanandhan and the Mumbai Police, as a team, succeeded in bringing this number down to zero for the next 11 years. He succeeded in reestablishing the feeling of safety among people. As peace was restored, the hotel industry flourished, the building industry flourished and all other industrial activity grew.

The commercial capital of India, which had almost come to a standstill, once again became a booming finance center. That year, to acknowledge the success of the Crime Branch in eliminating organized crime in Mumbai, the state of Maharashtra awarded eight President's Police Medals for Meritorious Services to the team members, while Sivanandhan was awarded a President's Police Medal for Distinguished Services.

Out of the eight police medals that were given in the year 2000, seven were received by Sivanandhan and his team as Joint CP, Crime.

The seven people who received these medals were:

1. D Sivanandhan, Jt CP (Crime)

2. AD Shinde, DCP (Economic Offence Wing)

3. SJ Inamdar, Inspector, Crime Branch

4. VK Navghare, Inspector, Crime Branch

5. MD Javed Rahid, Inspector, Crime Branch

6. AM Darekar, Head Constable, badge no 18591

7. BA Gadge, Head Constable, badge no 14833

They had outperformed expectations. They had delivered results.

Now he could recall the lady on television and proudly say, "Madam, I hope you are happy and sure that your husband will come back home alive and not worry about him becoming a target of some local *goonda* or gangster."

Let us flash back to what the situation in Mumbai was like before Sivanandhan took over as Joint CP, Crime and the situation after that. Mumbai is a city where businesses flourish and people feel safe.

How was this done?

There was a six-pronged attack strategy on Mafia gangs:

▶ Detentions

▶ Extortionists detained

▶ Gangsters arrested

▶ Firearms seized

▶ Police operations

▶ MCOCA arrests

Let us look at some statistics to get a clear indication of the situation based on the above strategy.

▶ Extortion cases

In the period 1998-2001, for a total of 1,229 extortion cases, there were 1,651 detentions; which means that this was the period of the maximum number of detentions. Therefore, the number of extortion cases reduced from 728 in the year 1993 to 176 in the year 2009 and has been on the wane after that.

▶ Police operations

In the period 1998-2001, 298 notorious criminals were neutralized in 238 police operations. The impact of this action was sustained for years.

▶ Shootout by criminals

In inter-rivalry gang wars, 192 criminals were eliminated in 176 incidents. In 2009, there have been only eight shootouts.

▶ Gangsters arrested

A total of 1,635 gangsters – a mind-boggling figure – were arrested in the period 1998-2001, bringing complete control over the underworld nexus. As a result, in 2009, only 66 criminals were arrested, while in 2012, only 38 gangsters were arrested. This clearly shows that the gangs began losing their grip over the city.

▶ MCOCA cases

After the MCOCA was implemented, in the period 1999-2001, in 53 cases, 214 gangsters were arrested. In 2009, this figure came down to 24 gangsters arrested in only five cases.

▶ Incidents of murders with firearms

Gangsters used to only murder people in broad daylight. The worst year was 1998, when in 93 incidents, 101 citizens were killed. Extortions were a common phenomenon. There were 367 cases of extortion and petty crimes reported, in which 32 film stars received extortion threats. To bring those criminals into custody in a single year, 640 arrests were done.

▶ Multi-pronged attack on Mafia gangs (complete statistics)

(Note: the figures in bold are indicative of the period when Sivanandhan was the Joint CP, Crime)

Year	1993	1994	1995	1996	1997	1998	1999	2000	2001	2002	2003	2004	2005	2006	2007	2008	2009
Detentions (MPDA)	172	116	129	353	144	**365**	**638**	**242**	**406**	281	165	137	190	186	151	80	61
Extortionists detained	69	48	51	176	91	**200**	**394**	**127**	**242**	192	117	37	42	26	27	23	22
Gangsters arrested	213	435	248	273	308	**455**	**437**	**348**	**395**	304	163	207	174	235	208	291	68
Firearms seized	386	286	248	226	269	**535**	**540**	**434**	**471**	343	564	466	506	355	399	311	314
Police operations	36	30	9	57	72	**48**	**83**	**73**	**94**	47	40	15	13	16	12	20	8
MCOC Arrests	—	—	—	—	—	**—**	**64**	**65**	**85**	31	12	90	134	123	52	80	28

Source: Crime Branch, Mumbai Police

▶ Working with ethics and reliability

To prove leadership, you must have moral superiority and become a role model; nobody should be able to accuse you of corruption or any other deviousness. The only focus of the leader should be the application of his mind to the job. If this integrity is maintained, the leader is respected in every transfer he gets, and even after he retires.

Prior to this stint in Mumbai, during 1995-98, Sivanandhan was the Deputy Inspector General (DIG) of Police in the Nagpur range, which included Nagpur, Chandrapur, Gadchiroli, Bhandara, Bondia and Wardha. The challenges he faced in this Naxal stronghold were completely different from heading the force in Mumbai.

In these Naxal-affected areas, his leadership style was completely different from what he later adopted in Mumbai. What worked in one place and time will not work in another. The leader has to create customized solutions for different challenges.

In these areas, policepersons were "class enemies", according to the Naxalites. Therefore, the police were ambushed and killed and landmines were used against them.

While killing gangsters in police operations could work in metros, Sivanandhan knew that such killings with Naxalites would backfire, because it was an ideologically driven insurgency or terrorism, as one can call it. Killing Naxalites like gangsters would result in the blooming of so many more thousands of Naxalites.

So, he thought of a different solution. He had able assistants along with other experienced team members. Together, they made a different action plan.

The strategy was to persuade people to surrender. At that time, the government was not giving them any financial assistance for surrendering. Only by good practices and good policing were Sivanandhan and his team able to handle the situation.

It was ensured that no unnecessary person was arrested; no innocent person was harassed and nobody was shot unnecessarily. Finally, the team was able to persuade all the Maharashtrians in the Naxal areas to surrender.

An example is of Shivaji Tumreddy and his wife. They surrendered with their AK-47 rifles along with ₹ 1.5–2 lakh of cash. They were not offered any money; they surrendered with money instead.

To achieve such results, you should trust others and also be trusted by others. This is a totally different strategy.

Naxalism continues to be a very serious problem in our country. But at least in Maharashtra, Sivanandhan was able to contribute in a major way to controlling it. By using strategic leadership and applying a different thought process, by the time Sivanandhan and others in their team left the Nagpur range, there was no Maharashtrian left in Naxal groups. The team was able to achieve at least that much.

An incident is worth mentioning here connected to Naxalism and moral standards.

During that tenure, a group of policepersons had set up camp in a particular area, where the Naxals were on the prowl. Through their night vision binoculars, the policepersons saw a group of villagers. In the green forests, the people were wearing green uniforms and had guns in their hands.

The policepersons thought they were Naxalites and challenged them. During the operations, one villager was shot. By the time the police realized he was not a Naxalite, it was too late. The police tried to evacuate this person, but before he could reach the hospital, he bled to death.

Now, the dilemma was whether the police should say they had killed a Naxalite or admit the fact that a common villager had been shot by mistake.

This was brought to Sivanandhan's notice over the phone. His clear direction was to call a press conference and admit that a poor villager had been shot due to mistaken identity.

Sivanandhan also had to take responsibility for the situation. He told the entire Nagpur range, consisting of the policepersons of seven districts, to contribute whatever they could, say a day's salary, to ensure the rehabilitation of the poor woman who had lost her husband. This woman was also given employment later.

These are two diametrically opposite examples. The main takeaway from both these is: leadership only matters. In fact, Sivanandhan's leadership in both these examples highlights the qualities of leadership described by Chanakya. Let's see how:

Intelligent and dynamic

When Sivanandhan took over the task of cracking down on the underworld in Mumbai, he had to do it intelligently, in a carefully planned manner, strategically using the legal means available to him. But good plans alone do not get results. You have to put your plan into action. We see Sivanandhan making an action plan and acting on the plan, which included imparting confidence in his team, providing them adequate resources and training and resolving the issues that plagued the team. Finally, we see Mumbai safe and thriving.

Retired Assistant Commissioner of Police, Dashrath Avhad, who worked with Sivanandhan in the Crime Branch says, "Sivanandhan was one of the finest officers in the Maharashtra police force. He was a dynamic leader and always handled a crisis situation by leading from the front. Dealing with the gangsters was not easy, but Sivanandhan was a true leader and never let his officers down."

Associates with elders

While Sivanandhan was making an action plan, he consulted elders (experts) from various fields. For instance, he frequently met and drew inspiration from senior police officers such as Sarva Shri KF Rustomji, Julio Rebeiro, VK Saraf, SV Bhave, S Ramamurthy, SK Bapat, Satish Sahney, Arvind Inamdar and MR Reddy, among others.

Truthful in speech

Sivanandhan's response to the shooting of the poor villager who was mistaken as a Naxalite is a case in point. Sivanandhan had the opportunity to conceal the facts and declare the person a Naxalite, which is in fact, a common practice in such cases. However, he accepted the mistake and was truthful in speech.

Does not break promises

The biggest promise you give is to yourself. We find Sivanandhan was happy that the promise to ensure security to the people was delivered. He could recall the lady on television who was fearful for her husband's life and be assured that he had succeeded in quelling her fears. He did not break the promise he had made to himself.

Grateful

Sivanandhan was always grateful to the people who supported him in achieving his objectives, be it his team members, the senior officials who empowered him, lawyers or other experts. He maintains that all success was possible due to team effort. With this humility, one rises in his career too. Otherwise, he would not have risen to the position of Director General of Police.

Desirous of training

Sivanandhan is a person who is always ready to learn and explore. Post the 26/11 Mumbai terror attack, his task was to create world-class security systems and processes in India. He even invited Israeli specialists and experts from IB (Intelligence Bureau) and other Central police organizations. This shows his eagerness to learn from other experts. Wherever he worked during his years of service, Sivanandhan invited experts such as Prof Rooshikumar Pandya, NH Atreya, Om Kaul, Smt Jaya Rao, Swami Sukhbodananda and other motivational speakers to give lectures to police officers.

Easily approachable

Shivaji Tumreddy and his wife's surrender with their AK-47 rifles along with ₹ 1.5-2 lakh of cash was the result of Sivanandhan's able handling of the situation. This shows that people felt comfortable with him and could trust him. Sivanandhan has the ability to connect to the common man. Even when someone meets him for the first time, it is evident how easily approachable he is and he would immediately address their problems and concerns. This is an important quality for a leader.

★ KEYS TO LEADERSHIP ★

1. Boost the morale of your people: They will look upon you for that.

2. Think out of the box: Be ready to experiment.

3. Have high moral standards: Personal integrity is the key.

4. Give resources to people: Money, tools and techniques are required for every operation.

5. Admit mistakes: Do not try to cover them up.

The Leader in Me

Chapter 2

Amatya

THE MINISTER/MANAGER

Swami	the king
Amatya	**the minister**
Janpada	the country
Durg	the fortified city
Kosha	the treasury
Dand	the army
Mitra	the ally

PART A

THE SECOND SECRET

Amatya: The Manager

IN THE ARTHASHASTRA, the importance of a minister is emphasized repeatedly. In fact, Chapter 8 in Book 1 is titled *Amatyautpatti*, meaning "appointment of ministers".

Who is an *amatya*? He can be called a *mantri* or a minister. His counterpart in the corporate world is the manager. There is a difference, yet there are similarities between leaders and managers. Depending on the context, every leader is a manager for someone and every manager is a leader for someone else.

Let us take an example. The CEO of a company is the leader. If the vice-president (VP) of the company manages a part of the work for the CEO, the VP becomes the minister or manager. However, the VP is also a leader to his team members. His subordinates, such as the assistant vice-president, become his ministers.

Similarly, the CEO is the manager or the minister for the chairman of the company. He reports to the company board and manages the organization.

A person who manages a hotel as an employee is the husband and head of the family at home. Thus, he is a leader in his home. A person working in the IT department of a company may not have to worry about company finances. But when he has to manage a family at home, he has to understand the basic concepts of finance to pay the bills and manage expenses. Therefore, all managers are leaders and all leaders are managers in different contexts.

In this chapter, we will discuss the qualities of a minister, whom we will call a manager. You can work towards developing these qualities to become successful in life.

Before we do that, let us look at why companies require managers, or why a king requires his *amatya* or ministers. That will also explain why a management degree is in great demand today, why fresh management graduates get such high salaries and rewarding opportunities and why business or B-schools are a flourishing industry.

In Book 1, Chapter 7, Verse 9 of the *Arthashastra*, Chanakya says,

"Rulership can be successfully carried out (only) with the help of associates. One wheel alone does not turn. Therefore, he (the ruler) should appoint ministers and listen to their opinion."

Let us delve deeper into this verse.

The help of associates: Look at the situation from the point of view of the king. He has to manage a large kingdom, which is impossible to do alone. Anyone who thinks he can do it all by himself can never grow in life. Leaders know the importance of teamwork.

In the olden days, the king had associates in the form of his friends, advisors, teachers, mentors and seniors. In India, we have the concept of the king being advised by his gurus. These are strong associates.

One wheel alone does not turn: Chanakya gives an analogy here. If there is only one wheel in a bullock cart, the cart keeps going in circles. There is movement, but no progress. There is action, but no direction.

Vehicles that have to carry heavy cargo and lots of people have many wheels. The bigger the vehicle, more the wheels required and the stronger they should be. Heavy trucks sometimes have 40–50 wheels to transport heavy machinery.

Remember this: One wheel alone does not turn.

Appoint ministers: Therefore, Chanakya suggests appointing ministers. The number of ministers required depends on the size of the kingdom and the volume of responsibilities the king handles.

A similar situation exists in the business world. If a person owns a single hotel, only one manager may be required to manage it. But the owner of a chain of hotels may require many more to take care of the operations of each of the hotels, separately and collectively.

However, owners themselves are often managers. First-generation businessmen especially cannot understand the difference between owning and managing a business. Once you understand the difference, your business starts to flourish.

For example, the owner-manager of a restaurant will take customers' orders, make the bills and serve the customers. This is good for a start, when the owner must make efforts to learn the ground reality. But the next step is to get a manager who runs the show, so that the owner can focus on thinking about the future of the business.

The owner needs to think about business expansion, potential business opportunities, cost minimization, sources of manpower supply, customer satisfaction, profit maximization and other such areas. However, if he works in the restaurant every day from morning to evening, where is the time to think about these critical questions?

Therefore, appointing a manager who takes care of the details frees the owner for "thinking time". Leaders understand this. That is why they are leaders.

However, for that to happen, the first requirement is to trust your people. If you do not trust your managers, you will never delegate work to them, and will not have the time to become a leader.

An ability to trust others and others being able to trust you are important qualities a leader has to develop. Along with that, make sure you consider your managers as equals. Just because they report to you does not mean they are not intelligent or have to be treated disrespectfully.

In the previous chapter, we saw that one of the qualities of a leader is humility. Be grateful to your people and treat them with respect.

Listen to their opinion: Chanakya says, "Appoint ministers, and listen to their opinion."

After you have recognized the need for managers, the next step is to listen to them. Listening is different from hearing. It is an open-minded approach towards the other person while he is speaking.

Each of us is conditioned to think in a certain way. We build the realities of our life based on our experiences. But in listening, you give yourself a challenge to be ready to understand the other person. You acknowledge that both you and the other person may be right; or your reasoning may be wrong and the other person may be right. You open your mind to different possibilities.

Managers are not machines. They too are continuously thinking and applying their minds to the job. They may have insights that they want to share with you. They have a hold over ground realities; they are the eyes and ears of your organization. But all this experience is useless if you do not "listen" to their opinion.

In the industrial era, productivity was measured based on how many units were produced through machines each day. Speed was important. To achieve speed, one had to stop thinking and work mechanically. However, Toyota changed that when their focus became quality, rather than just quantity. Now, any person in the assembly line was permitted to reject the product if the quality was not found satisfactory. The product did not need to reach the Quality Control department for the final inspection and the decision to accept or reject. Every person in the assembly line, therefore, became a "thinking" person whose opinion was respected.

Today's world is one of ideas and innovation. Therefore, the leader must listen to the opinions of his managers. This time-tested formula of Chanakya is relevant today in every situation.

When the king faces a problem, he is supposed to discuss it with his ministers and then take a decision.

You must have heard the saying, "A king is as good as the advice he gets." In today's situation too, you need to take inputs from the people in your team before taking the final call. These ministers and managers help you to think from various perspectives, which you may overlook if you are analyzing a problem alone.

The police system too has its *amatyas*. As a Commissioner of Police, Sivanandhan had his managers in the form of DCPs (Deputy Commissioners of Police) handling various zones. He would call meetings with them on a regular basis and use their information and insights to learn about what was happening in the city.

This helped him build his knowledge base. He took every report and every piece of information seriously and integrated information given by the various DCPs to get a complete picture. He also had his own informers to cross-verify the facts. The key was to keep an open mind and respect each piece of information that flowed to him, directly or indirectly.

Had it not been for his effective and efficient "ministers" who stood by him during testing times, Sivanandhan would not have been successful in his career.

A king can never be complete without his ministers. And a minister is never complete without a king. They are interdependent, like reflections of each other. Their rapport with each other contributes to an organization's rapid growth. Their mutual trust is the push required to achieve results.

Also, it is important to note that every manager has the potential to become a leader. And every leader was a good manager in the past. You start as a good follower to become a good leader.

Take a break now and think about what you have read so far.

This book encourages you to "think", as according to Chanakya, thinking is the first quality a leader has to develop. This method of thinking is called *Aanvikshiki*, which also means philosophy and an intelligent person.

As you take a break, here is a question to think about: How much time in a day do you spend in thinking? Do you have a dedicated time in your daily routine only to think?

Thinking about thinking, makes you a great leader.

PART B

ACCORDING TO CHANAKYA

Management

THE ARTHASHASTRA FOLLOWS the unique and interesting method of using *sutras* (verses) to teach. These brilliant one-liners are full of deep insights. So too, is the case with defining management in Book 1, Chapter 15, Verse 42:

"The means of starting undertakings, the excellence of men and material, (suitable) apportionment of place and time, provision against failure (and) accomplishment of work – this is deliberation (management) in its five aspects".

In this one-liner, Chanakya defines the five principles of management:

1. The means of starting undertakings (assignments/projects)

2. Excellence of men and materials

3. Suitable place and time

4. Provision against failure

5. Accomplishment of work

All management theories and concepts are based on certain principles. These are the basic foundations on which we evaluate the efficiency of the manager, the productivity of the organization and its success in achieving objectives. Voluminous books are available to define and describe management.

However, Chanakya has given the most refined view of management in a single verse.

Let us look at the five principles of management defined by Chanakya.

▶ The Means of Starting Undertakings (Assignments/Projects)

Every organization needs projects or assignments to manage and complete. However, the best manager is one who not only takes up a project given by his supervisor, but also creates projects on his own. Stephen Covey in his book, *The Seven Habits of Highly Effective People* describes this as being "proactive". This is an important quality for a good leader and a good manager.

▶ Excellence of Men and Materials

A manager has access to resources, which are to be used at his discretion in order to accomplish tasks. These are the people who work under his direction and the tools used by him and his team. A good manager must be able to make his team highly productive and ensure optimum utilization of materials like machinery, space, budgets, etc.

▶ Suitable Place and Time

Management is about deciding the right place and the right time to make your move. Like in warfare, timing is very crucial. When to attack the enemy is not an easy question to answer. It requires careful planning, analysis and also patience. This sense of the right "timing" comes from one's own experience, knowledge and guidance from other sources.

▶ Provision against Failure

Every move has to be carefully planned taking two alternatives into consideration: the best-case scenario of success and the worst-case scenario of total failure. A backup plan is required in each move. One needs to be prepared with alternative solutions in case of failures. A businessman was once asked the reason for his success, to which he replied, "I take into consideration failures at each stage. I plan alternative moves even before I start the venture." It is like having Plan A, Plan B and Plan C in place.

▶ Accomplishment of Work

Finally, management is about achieving results. It is very important to have parameters to check whether you have achieved what you set out to do. Every project is started with a certain objective in mind. The process may evolve as the project is executed, but finally, the target has to be achieved, even if the route taken to reach there is different from what was initially planned.

▶ Qualities of a Good Manager According to Chanakya

The professional man is in essence, one who provides service. It is a service that wells up from the entire complex of his personality. In a very real sense, his professional service cannot be separate from his personal being. He has no goods to sell, no land to till, his only asset is himself.

If he does not contain the quality of integrity, he is worthless. If he does, he is priceless. The value is either nothing or it is infinite.

So, do not try to set a price on yourselves. Do not debase yourselves by equating your souls to what they will bring in the market.

Like love, talent is useful only in its expenditure and is never exhausted.

Certain it is that man must eat. So, set what price you must on your service. But, never confuse the performance, which is great, with the compensation, be it money, power or fame.

— Judge Elbert P. Tuttle

The professional man is indeed of great value in every organization. The professional manager in today's organizations should also reflect the qualities of integrity and service-oriented action. His only asset is himself.

We have seen in the previous chapter that the leader has to be self-motivated and inspiring. He is a solid rock that stands in the midst of the storm around. He is the lighthouse that gives direction to others. He is the silver lining in the dark cloud.

The manager – Chanakya's *amatya* – also needs to possess these qualities and more. So, let us go once again to the *Arthashastra* and look at the qualities of an ideal minister.

In Book 6, Chapter 1, Verses 4-6, Chanakya states that the qualities of an *amatya* are:

▶ Desire to learn

▶ Power of retention

▶ Thorough understanding

▶ Intentness on truth

▶ Ability to lead an army

▶ Sweetness of speech

To understand these qualities and their significance, you should visualize yourself in a managerial position. Do you possess these qualities? If not, how can you develop these?

Also note that when you compare the qualities of a leader and manager, you will find many similarities. As stated above, they are reflections of each other.

▶ Desire to learn

A leader is supposed to learn continuously; so should a manager. Without continuous learning, there is stagnation in a manager's career and boredom sets in. In offices, there is often rejoicing at the thought, "Thank God, it's Friday!" Why? Does God differentiate between Sunday and Monday? Does the sun say, "Because it is Sun-day today, I will shine brighter and on other days, I will not do my work?"

When you get stuck in a routine, are trapped in fixed ways of thinking and doing things, and there is no new knowledge or learning, boredom is bound to set in. Then, you require breaks, weekends and vacations.

This is not to say that you should not have holidays and time with family and friends. But every day can be a day of celebration; your Monday can be as beautiful as Saturday or Sunday.

Ever since the age of 27, when I started on my own journey of becoming an entrepreneur, I have forgotten the difference between weekdays and weekends.

Every day is a celebration because every day, I am learning. And I have never got bored of myself. I hate the days when I have no work to do. That does not mean I am a workaholic. I love my work and find joy in it. I read books, listen to music, watch movies and go on long drives with my friends and family.

A manager can also achieve this if work is not considered a "task" to be completed, but an opportunity to learn. One may think it is easy when you are the owner of a company or your own boss. This is not true. I know people who are not owners but professionals and managers. But they do not live their lives from one weekend to the next, one increment to the next or one job to the next.

They have the desire to learn. They work very hard and learn a lot. They learn by reading official reports, listening to others, traveling or resolving a problem in their companies. They draw on the experience of seniors and juniors, their children, families, friends and their mentors. They learn from professional journals, newspapers, television channels, radio, plays and movies; and from meetings, seminars and professional courses. They imbibe life lessons from watching the sunrise, a passing cloud or the movement of an ant. Because they have a learning mindset, they learn from anything and everything.

The whole universe becomes their university. And in that state of mind, they become deep thinkers, meditative in nature, and are able to find solutions to complex problems.

▶ **Power of retention**

Someone asked me in a seminar, "What is the greatest problem in our life?" "Not being able to remember and apply the knowledge you have when the time comes," was my instant reply.

In ancient Indian scriptures, there are many stories where a brilliant student is cursed by his teacher, "When the time to apply the knowledge comes, you will forget it!" This was also the curse given to Karna, one of the greatest warriors in the *Mahabharata*, by his guru, Parashurama, when the latter found out that Karna had lied to him.

As a result, Karna's rival Arjuna, who was less skilled than him, killed him. Karna was an expert in military warfare, but could not recollect what he wanted at the right time and had to lose his life.

Therefore, to retain knowledge and recollect it when it is "really" required is a skill a manager has to develop. Swami Chinmayananda said this jovially, "Before the exams I am wise, after the exams I am wise, but during the exams I am other-wise."

Retention is not just memory skills or reproducing what you have learnt. It is going into your past database, selecting what is really required, diagnosing the current problem, choosing what is relevant and making an action plan, in the shortest possible time. Fighter pilots have to decide in a split second. Policemen have to take a call for action here and now.

Have you ever faced an instance in your life when you were all alone in a very difficult situation, and when all your training, knowledge from books you had read and all the advice you had received came handy in that very moment of judgement?

That is retention in the true sense. That is wisdom in action. No reference time, no consulting time, no brainstorming activity is possible. There is only you and the moment of truth. You take that key decision and jump into the fire and the unknown power in you awakens. The leader in you is born.

▶ Thorough understanding

Understanding has to be thorough and complete. We find young lovers often saying "I love you", but these are superficial words. Real love comes from understanding one another completely and unconditionally. An old couple really understands the meaning of love. When the old man is hungry, his wife understands. He does not have to ask for food. When she is upset, he understands. There is perfect mental tuning between the two.

In the same way, there has to be thorough understanding between the leader and the manager. It does not come from day one. It requires time being spent with each other, working with each other for a long period of time. But when this understanding reaches its maturity, there are no communication gaps any more, no "whys" and "ifs", no complaints of "he did it, not me". There is only silence and a deep sense of calmness between the two.

The king and the minister, or the leader and the manager, have to reach that level of maturity. They work together for a higher purpose. They strive together to achieve a common goal. They may disagree on the methods and have different points of view, but their objective is not forgotten.

Disagreement between two people does not mean they do not understand each other. In fact, Santrupt Misra from the Aditya

Birla group said in the film *Chanakya Speaks*, "If the king and the minister agree on the same thing, then one is redundant." "Strength lies in differences not similarities," said the management guru, Stephen Covey.

▶ Intentness on truth

Truth is one, but it has various dimensions. A true manager will try to understand this complete truth. The story of the elephant and the five blind men is relevant here. While each blind man touched a different part of the elephant and described it differently as a pillar, broom, fan, wall and so on, the person with eyesight said, "All of you are right from your standpoint, yet the elephant is very different." Each had his limited perspective, but missed the big picture. It required the wisdom of a person with full vision to see the complete truth.

A manager needs to develop this "big picture" vision. Many people will provide different perspectives to a given problem or situation. He needs to gather all this information and collate it into a larger story. In this process, the truth is discovered.

Good managers have to be aware of and respect the perspectives of different individuals. But their intentness has to be on the truth, ensuring that the objective is not forgotten.

Intentness on truth also means the ability to take the next step. If you have reached the conclusion that a certain action is required after arriving at the truth, as a manager, you need to implement your findings.

For example, Mahatma Gandhi was convinced that non-violence was the way to freedom. But no one would accept his theory if it did not lead to results. He had to demonstrate his "experiments with truth" in thought and action. He did that through his role in India's freedom struggle, and attained fame and respect in India and the world. He said, "My life is my message."

> ▶ Ability to lead an army

A manager has a team that executes tasks. The minister has to ensure that his team implements the king's decision. But the team members will do that only if they accept the minister or manager himself as their leader.

Therefore, a manager or minister has to be an inspiring leader.

True leadership is inspirational. A manager cannot tell his supervisor, "My team does not listen to me; please help." A manager is a leader, and therefore, cannot complain.

Leadership is never demanded, but commanded. Authority should never be imposed; people should accept it voluntarily.

You should be like the pied piper. Your team should be mesmerized by the music of your vision and be ready to do anything at your command. This is charismatic leadership. This is transformational leadership. These are the qualities a manager also needs to develop.

Remember the famous saying, "People do not leave organizations; they leave their bosses." That is, the boss was not inspirational enough to make them stick to their companies.

Be the manager who has the ability to lead a team like an army fired up to take up any challenge. The manager in you has to transform into a leader.

> ▶ Sweetness of speech

Sweetness of speech does not mean being nice to everyone. It is almost impossible to be so in the police force while handling law and order, terrorism and organized crime. One cannot be uniformly sweet. But wherever it is possible, it is important to keep it simple, to communicate the most complex problems in a simple manner to the people through the media and the police force.

Not all people in an organization have the ability to understand what the leader is thinking. The manager plays a very critical role here. The manager is the bridge between the senior management or board of directors, and the staff and laborers. The manager is like the filling in a sandwich. And in a sandwich, it is the filling that makes the difference.

In the same way, the manager has to be the sweet filling. He has the responsibility to convey what the organization needs to the last man. Until each person in your team is connected to the vision of the organization, they will not perform.

In the police force, the constable is given the same training about the Constitution of India that is given to the Director General of Police. This connects the first and the last person in the team for a common purpose.

On the other side, the problems of the staff and the foot soldiers also need to be conveyed to the senior management. Here too, the manager plays a critical role. The ability to present the problems of your team with a solution to the senior management and to get an approval is a skill in itself, be it getting a budget approved for a project or organizing a picnic. Getting that done and making your team happy is an essential part of management and leadership.

In the following chapters, you will see examples of how Sivanandhan got his team in the police force to work for him. But for that, he had to get many projects sanctioned by the home minister and government. To do that, he had to be a good communicator as well.

Truth is important, but the ability to communicate the truth in a palatable way is more important.

PART C

LEADERSHIP IN ACTION

Managing the 2 Lakh Police Force

AS A LEADER, Sivanandhan's job was to manage the strong force of 2 lakh policemen and policewomen in Maharashtra. He was a leader for the police force; while for the government, he was a manager whose task was to manage law and order. He worked for the government of Maharashtra for the best part of his life and retired at the senior-most position of Director General of Police (DGP) of the state.

Sivanandhan admits, "When I look back at such a career, I cannot thank the various government officials, politicians and other bureaucrats at the local, state, national level enough for the immense support I got from them. I am so overwhelmed by the results that given a chance, I would like to work all over again in the same police force."

Most IPS officers are highly intelligent people who made the choice to enter public life. They have been given world-class training to run and manage huge workforces. Their task as a leader and a manager can be compared to that of running a multinational organization. However, the challenges are immense as compared to what one would encounter in a corporate career.

Sivanandhan speaks about how he managed such challenges. "For me 'real management' starts with 'personnel management' and to 'accept change' as it comes. And being imaginative and ready for changes. Resisting change is something that stops us from growth."

Let us see how Sivanandhan's experiences as a leader and a manager embody the qualities of a good manager, as described by Chanakya.

▸ Desire to learn

One of the biggest challenges is dealing with the drastic changes that come with transfers. Unlike in a corporate career, where you know your company and your boss, where you are in a position to even interview and recruit your subordinates; in an IPS officer's case, everything is unknown. He may simply be informed one fine morning about his transfer from a metro city to the jungles of a Naxalite area and may have no idea about the culture or environment of the new place.

The political authorities in the new place may be different from those in the previous posting. They may be from a different party or background. The immediate senior to whom the officer would report may get transferred or promoted himself. The subordinates may have been working in the area for over 20 years, while the area would be completely new for this officer.

Moreover, the officer's family too has to adapt to such transfers. The time given to vacate the current house and join the new place of posting is very short. This brings a set of challenges for the family. The transfer order is not just a piece of paper, but an instruction that can have an impact on every aspect of life. In an officer's career, transfers may sometimes be decided by the seniors. At other times, the officer may have to take decisions related to the transfers of thousands of men and women who are his subordinates.

However, the police force is trained to face and accept this reality. Those who accept every new challenge and posting with a smile are never affected. They deliver results in every place they go. It is like making a completely new painting every time, because the canvas itself is new. To manage that, you have to be an artist and a strategist at the same time.

By the brush of your past experience, and the various colors of a completely new team, you start to approach the empty canvas – your new posting – with a fresh outlook and a hope to transform the place that you go to.

When a police officer goes to a new place, the challenge is not only for the officer, but also for the people working there. They may wonder about the officer and his agenda. He is like a foreign body in an existing system. There is initial resistance, which is natural. But if the officer becomes the positive change agent at every place, by the time the officer leaves, the people there hope he could have stayed back a little longer. That is the best gift for any officer while departing from his posting or retiring from his career.

Sivanandhan remarks, "In my tenure of 36 years in the service, I never lost my balance even for a single moment when the news of transfers came. I was ever ready to pack my bag with the family to an unknown, yet positive future. I was transferred 20 times and changed 26 houses." This experience made Sivanandhan and his family strong and adaptable. It also helped them learn new languages, acquaint themselves with new ethnic groups and cultures.

Despite his numerous transfers, he had the ability to learn from the experiences in every transfer. Thus, he could perfect his management and leadership skills every time there was a new posting or transfer. Apart from managing these personal challenges, the officer's main task is to manage the workforce at any new posting.

In the police force, one of the greatest challenges is administration. As a government department, administration is a huge machine that operates as the backbone. If you have ever visited a police station, you would have witnessed the administrative challenges the department faces.

There is lack of resources such as stationery, photocopiers and computers. Even though administrative reforms are taking place, the pace is very slow. While there is talk about e-governance and paperless offices, the ground reality is very different. Even though the use of technology is encouraged, the policeman who is on duty for 12 hours hardly gets time to attend new courses to upgrade his technology skills.

However, as a management researcher, I personally believe that efficient administration starts with the leader and the manager in charge. It is not just about paperwork; it is about attitude in that particular office. Especially in government offices, if the person in charge decides to help you, the problem can be resolved in a matter of minutes. If not, you will not get the required paper or permission for years. If the IPS or IAS officer decides to do so, he can transform the whole place. Otherwise, it is just another posting and the officer can give excuses such as "Our systems are like that; what can I do?"

Sivanandhan's desire to learn came handy here as well. It is to his credit that he made it a point throughout his career to simplify the administration process for the common man. He believed in world-class administration and even obtained world-class systems and process certifications as well as ISO certifications for many of the institutions that he created. He got eight police stations in Thane city accredited with ISO certifications. Standard operating processes (SOPs) were adopted at these institutions, which will be beneficial for generations to come.

When he was in charge of the immigration process for four years (1987–91), his biggest achievement was changing the atmosphere of that office from a typical police office with "No, No" all the time to "Yes, Yes" all the way. Sivanandhan was able to help millions of people get their passports, visas and various registrations. In fact, all the foreigners who were here would get their visa extensions through him. That not only brought him into the limelight, but a lot of these people also became his friends.

The Special Branch 2 office located behind St Xavier's College, in Mumbai, used to look like a regular government office, overflowing with dusty files which could not be retrieved at will. There was no visitors' room. This was the office where all foreigners residing in Mumbai would get their visa extension and residential permits. It created a very bad impression on the expats. So, the first thing Sivanandhan did was to change the look of the office by creating a visitors' room equipped with proper furniture and a reception desk managed by well-trained women staff. He also created a proper record room where all the files were neatly stacked and could be easily retrieved. On the ground floor, he created an easily accessible "one window system" where all short-term extensions were granted within 24 hours.

Earlier, visa extensions were granted for three months only and all foreigners had to surrender their residential permit (RP) at airport immigration, every time they traveled. Now, Sivanandhan arranged for a proper RP that looked more like a passport and allowed them to retain their RPs so that they did not need to come and collect them after every trip. The foreigners were allowed long-term extensions too, so the number of visitors hanging around the office reduced to a great extent. For the first time, office records were computerized.

Several incidents from this tenure of Sivanandhan's are worth mentioning. Once, he received intimation that some Japanese Red Army girls would pass through the airport. Sivanandhan personally led the team to identify and challenge the girls. The team found that five Mizoram girls were carrying brown sugar to Madrid using fake Japanese passports! When confronted with a Japanese traveler asking them questions, the truth spilled out. Checking their baggage revealed 60 kilos of contraband.

There was another occasion where an assassin allegedly belonging to the Abu Nidal group had illegally entered Mumbai and opened fire with deadly UZI guns on the Air France crew inside their bus. He had also hurled live hand grenades inside the bus. The pilot was shot in the stomach, but the assailant was caught by two daring immigration officers at the Sahar international airport. Sustained interrogation resulted in the conviction of the foreigner under TADA.

Sivanandhan created a special investigation cell with handpicked officers and they detected around 350 Sri Lankans every year trying to migrate to European countries with false passports. Many Indians trying to migrate to the USA with fake passports were detected by a special squad. The US government was so happy that they sent a deputy secretary, James Warden, to personally appreciate and convey the US government's gratitude.

Sivanandhan arranged many special training sessions for the immigration officers, including training on soft skills like welcoming foreigners in their mother tongue, giving them quick clearance and arranging a special handout that would give them complete directions on the rules and regulations.

The mammoth effort put in by the immigration staff during the evacuation of a large number of Indians from Kuwait during the war is unforgettable.

The police office has a corporate ambience even now, where officers wear a tie and are ever willing to help with a smile. At the airport too, things have vastly improved.

When Sivanandhan was Additional Commissioner of Police (crime), computerization was another major achievement. In fact, ₹ 2.5 crore was spent on linking the entire Mumbai police network into one unit. Another great achievement is updating all crime records. Thus, criminal information, which was earlier maintained manually, has been computerized and is now part of institutional memory.

Sivanandhan also ensured the smooth functioning of internal administration throughout his career, which included making sure that salaries were disbursed on time, and postings and promotions were not delayed. This made a huge impact on the overall efficient functioning of the system and boosted the morale of the police force.

▶ **Power of retention**

Apart from ensuring that the systems work well, the leader and manager needs to connect to people at a personal level too. The human touch is required while managing an office. Human beings cannot live in isolation and need to be recognized and appreciated.

One of the challenges for the Western world is the individualistic culture. Once, when I was travelling abroad a native citizen told me, "If someone meets with an accident, our traffic monitoring system is so good that an ambulance will arrive in less than two minutes." "In fact, no one is inconvenienced because they know help is on its way."

Sivanandhan describes how he made the human touch possible. He made it a point to remember the names of the people in his team. "I used to call everyone by name. I made an effort to remember everyone by their first name. One may wonder if it is possible to remember the names of a police force as large at 2 lakh? No way. I am not advocating that each of us should become master computers in memorizing names of people. But you can at least make the effort to memorize the names of the few people directly reporting to you." There is a saying that the sweetest sound to any person is his own name. Remembering the names of people who work with you is a good practice.

He fondly recollects attending the marriage of a young constable who worked with him in Mumbai. Sivanandhan came all the way from Nagpur to attend this wedding. The cop's joy knew no bounds when he saw his old boss sitting in the front row.

▶ Thorough understanding

The people who directly report to you are your *amatyas*.

Sivanandhan followed a simple policy when it came to his *amatyas* and the police force, "I will train them so well that they will manage the law and order situation well and effectively handle crime control."

Sivanandhan had a thorough understanding of what human beings want. When a person is not worried about the basic necessities, he will focus on his work and deliver results. Receiving the salary on time, housing, food and children's education are important matters to every person. When you manage this, they manage your work.

Sivanandhan subsidized the education for policepersons' children, created safe police stations, created schools at Thane and even in Naxal-affected areas like Gadchiroli, Chandrapur and many more.

Thus, his employees thought of him as a leader, who took care of them, who understood their problems and offered solutions; who didn't just talk, but took action.

People do not understand what is in your mind and heart. They understand what you deliver, what you do for them. If you create an environment where they are being taken care of, employees also work with more commitment.

▶ Intentness on truth

There is no point beating around the bush when the time has come to deliver. Sivanandhan had to take tough calls in handling criminals and even his own men. He had the ability to call a spade a spade. If it was required, he would also suspend or dismiss members of his own team.

Dashrath Avhad, retired ACP adds, "Officers who did not have a good conduct were transferred so as to facilitate smooth functioning of the Crime Branch."

Sivanandhan once dismissed a Senior Inspector under Section 311 of the Constitution. He explains, "Just like a cancerous growth in a body part must be removed, team members who have become like cancerous growths must be removed to ensure the health and effectiveness of the team."

▶ Ability to Lead an Army

The next step is to empower your subordinates to take charge. A good leader never withholds power. He understands that true power comes from empowering others. Today, the buzzword is decentralization. Government and public organizations also grow by not restricting the juniors, but allowing them to take spot decisions. The toe has to be as important as the head. In today's world, where information is available at the speed of thought, it is important that your subordinates also take quick decisions.

However, to take up the responsibility when things go wrong, and to accept the mistakes of the juniors as your mistakes, is leadership.

Sivanandhan says, "When my team was executing shootouts of gangsters, I was empowering them to take immediate decisions. I also had to give them the courage and confidence that I am with you – that moral support is required."

▶ Sweetness of speech

Sivanandhan had the ability to communicate in a pleasant and effective manner, whether with his subordinates, the press or his seniors. Being sweet does not mean using sugar-coated words. It means the ability to deliver the truth tactfully and effectively.

When certain approvals are needed, such as for the application of new rules, effective communication about the need for new rules is necessary. Sivanandhan's success in communication can be gauged by the number of new policies he introduced for his team and the police force throughout his career.

Another example of pleasant and effective communication is from the time when Sivanandhan was a police chief. He recollects that a lady came to him once and was asked to take a chair. She refused. When he insisted, she said, "Sir, how can I sit in front of you?" "What is the problem?" he asked. Lowering her voice, she said, "Sir, I am in the profession of selling my body. I am not equal to you in status." He said "Until you sit down and have a cup of tea, I will not listen to you." She had come to complain of her husband ill-treating her. By putting her at ease and talking to her respectfully, Sivanandhan was able to help her.

Various people came to him with various problems — there were film stars, rich business tycoons, community leaders and even college students. He had an open-door policy and treated everyone with respect. That is how Sivanandhan managed his team and his work.

★ TIPS FOR GOOD MANAGEMENT ★

1. Be prepared for change: Never resist new assignments or projects.

2. Manage yourself first: Self-management is important for managing others.

3. Ensure good administration: Systems and processes should be in place.

4. Know people by name: It provides the personal touch.

5. Empower people: Encourage your subordinates to take decisions.

The Leader in Me

Chapter 3

Janpada

THE CITIZENS/CUSTOMERS

Swami	the king
Amatya	the minister
Janpada	**the country**
Durg	the fortified city
Kosha	the treasury
Dand	the army
Mitra	the ally

THE THIRD SECRET

Janpada: Citizens or Customers

GOOD GOVERNANCE HAS been explained as, "Till the last man in the last village is not happy, the work of the government is not done." Similarly, until every citizen is not feeling safe and secure, the work of the police is not complete.

Once, King Chandragupta Maurya was thinking about the fact that everything in his life was now directed and controlled by Chanakya. His daily timetable of what to do, who to meet, what food to eat, and even the important decision of who to marry was decided by his guru.

Chandragupta did not seem to have a personal life at all. In utter frustration, he told Chanakya one day that he would not listen to him. He wanted his personal space and independence. Though he was a king, he was also an individual with personal desires. He asked Chanakya why everything he did, public or personal, was controlled.

Chanakya reminded his able student, "There are two categories of people in this world who are not blessed with personal happiness — the king and the teacher. Till every person in the kingdom is not happy, both cannot take rest."

This may seem like a strong statement for a leader — no personal life at all. But note that Chanakya, the guru, imposes this rule even on himself.

Both the king and the guru are supposed to dedicate their life to the welfare of society. Most training programs in companies talk about work-life balance. But, the fact is that a leader should not differentiate between work and life.

At a breakfast meeting with Jagdish Seth, the renowned management guru and an advisor to some of the most prominent world leaders, we were talking about leadership. He too emphasized, "There cannot be any difference between personal and public life for a leader in today's world, especially with the media following him closely. Personal integrity is important in all spheres of life. When that happens, there is no internal conflict in the leader's mind and he is able to perform better and stay focused on the job."

Leadership has to be practiced 24 hours a day, 7 days a week, 365 days a year. It is a lifelong commitment.

That is why leadership is not only about what you are in public, but also what you are when the public is not around. It is being true to your conscience.

A leader will have his or her personal life, but it cannot be hidden from the public eye. This is because the leader sets an example; he becomes a role model. Therefore, the saying "*Yatha raja, tatha praja*" (As the leader, so the citizens).

We now come to the third aspect and the most important part of leadership: *Janpada*.

The Janpada are the citizens of the country. Without them, the kingdom is not complete. What is a country without people or a leader without followers? What is a king if there is no one for him to govern?

In the context of the corporate world, *Janpada* refers to customers or clients. The prime duty of a company is to serve its customers well. "The customer is king," says a popular marketing statement. Gandhiji also put it well:

"A customer is the most important visitor on our premises. He is not dependent on us. We are dependent on him. He is not an interruption in our work. He is the purpose of it. He is not an outsider in our business. He is part of it. We are not doing him a favor by serving him. He is doing us a favor by giving us an opportunity to do so."

The key question is whether you have served your customers well and taken care of them. Most companies today have customer service departments. Initially, customer service focused on selling products or services, but today, after-sales service is a more important component. In an open economy, providing good customer service is critical, because customers are aware of the service levels your competitors offer. Therefore, retaining customers becomes a big challenge if your customer service is not what it should be.

For a leader, it is important to be in touch with the customers on a regular basis. If you can think like the customer, you will be a good market leader in your business.

Even in governance, the challenge is to understand how citizens think. If you are able to understand their likes and dislikes, habits, culture, value systems, needs and aspirations, and give them what they need, you do not need to worry about your performance in the next elections.

Many politicians, who have understood this psychology of citizens, are able to win in the elections again and again. Even their future generations continue to win in the elections. This is not due to fooling the people by giving false promises. It is the ability to give the people what they want, without them having to ask for it.

To become a leader, one should understand how a leader thinks. And to understand how a leader thinks, one should understand how the citizens think.

The same thought is reiterated in the *Mahabharata*, when Bhishma advises Yudishthira on good governance. He says, "The king should be focused on his subjects, not the throne. If the subjects don't exist, the throne will also not exist."

What should the attitude of a king be?

In Book 1, Chapter 19, Verse 34 of the *Arthashastra*, Chanakya says:

"In the happiness of the subjects lies the happiness of the king, and what is beneficial to the subjects is his own benefit. What is dear to himself is not beneficial to the king, but what is dear to the subjects is beneficial to him."

All marketing theories or principles of good governance will find their culmination in this powerful saying. This most-quoted and well-accepted theory of Chanakya emphasizes that the happiness of the people is the happiness of the king.

Let us discuss the important aspects of this *sutra*.

▶ Happiness of subjects

To be happy is a great human achievement. Nations across the globe and world organizations like the United Nations have been working to define and understand the meaning of happiness to citizens.

Happiness has various dimensions — physical, mental and spiritual.

Physical: A person who is not physically fit cannot be happy. When you are unwell, happiness is far from your mind.

It is said that "Health is wealth." The World Health Organization (WHO) aims for happiness at this level for every citizen of the world.

The next level of physical happiness is the availability of adequate food and water. Nutritious food with good exercise keeps the body strong and fit.

Also required are bodily comforts. The external environment should be conducive to make you happy. If it is too hot, you need air-conditioning to feel comfortable. If it is too cold, you require warm clothes. If your chair is broken, you will not feel comfortable or happy.

Note that comforts at the physical level can be misunderstood as real happiness. As Swami Chinmayananda says, "You can be in luxury yet unhappy – luxuriously unhappy."

Therefore, the next aspect of happiness is mental happiness.

Mental: Happiness at the mental level is often called "mental health". A leader needs to understand that human beings have sentiments and feelings, and need to be emotionally taken care of. For this, a leader needs to develop emotional intelligence.

Increasing stress levels in modern-day living are a result of being mentally unhealthy. If mental health issues are not taken care of at the right time, a person can end up in an asylum or even commit suicide, as is evident from the increasing number of student suicides in our country.

Creating a caring and accepting atmosphere is required for mental health. At home, parents need to create an emotional bond with their children, so that they feel safe. Children should not be afraid to speak the truth or to face failures. The family should be able to instill confidence in the child, so that he or she can move beyond the failure and perform better.

In an organization, the leader should strive to create an environment that provides emotional security to employees and workers. In such an environment, mistakes are considered as learning steps, the individual is never blamed for failures and teamwork is given more importance than a one-man show. People get connected emotionally and the office becomes a second home. In many cases, people are so happy with their workplace that they do not complain about working extra hours.

Spiritual: This is the highest level of happiness and happiness in the real sense. If you are spiritually happy, nothing can move you. External problems do not matter to you, because such happiness comes from within and not from outside.

At the spiritual level, you are not dependent on physical, mental or intellectual activities. You are at peace with yourself. Even death cannot take away your happy state of being.

Once Death came to a spiritual master and said, "I am going to take you." The saint smiled, "I died long ago; you are only going to kill the body."

Spiritual happiness comes from the death of the ego, the biggest enemy in our lives. Once the ego is destroyed, nothing can stop us from being permanently happy.

In India, spiritual happiness has been emphasized since the dawn of time. Our history is full of stories of kings who even gave up their kingdoms in search of this true happiness. And leaders who have understood spiritual happiness become true leaders.

For India to fearlessly stand on its feet on the world platform, we need to connect to the spiritual foundations of our past. In leadership too, we need to take the highest leap — towards spiritual leadership.

We have seen that happiness has to be achieved at various levels, and for this to happen, the king or leader must understand all the dimensions of happiness. A leader cannot shirk his responsibility of providing physical happiness to his people in the form of food, clothing and shelter or ignore people's emotional well-being, on the pretext that real happiness is spiritual happiness. That is escaping from reality.

As parents take care of their children, the king must tend to his citizens. Children are first made comfortable at the physical level by giving them food and other material comforts; then at the mental and intellectual level by providing care, a house full of warm and loving people, followed by education and security. And finally, they are taught spiritual values that will help them stay strong through all the challenges of life.

In most underdeveloped and developing nations, the focus is on the physical component — food for all, housing, health, roads, security, jobs and so on. But the government's work does not end here. There are many economically developed nations, where suicide rates are high, social values have eroded and a sense of loneliness is prevalent. In such countries, while the citizens have achieved physical happiness, they have to progress to mental and spiritual happiness.

Once JRD Tata, ex-chairman of the Tata group of companies, was asked, "Do you want India to be an economic superpower?" Came back his landmark answer, "No, I want India to be a happy country!"

Today, India is in a very challenging situation after over six decades of independence. A part of our society is flourishing economically with good housing, education and jobs, and all the perks that come with them. However, a large part of the society is still struggling for basic survival. Initially it was about *roti, kapda aur makan* (food, clothing and shelter), now it is also about *bijlee, sadak aur paani* (power, roads and water).

The government is investing in projects to tackle these challenges, such as the *Sarva Shiksha Abhiyan* (basic primary and secondary education for all), rural health development programs, employment schemes and much more.

However, to ensure that India becomes a "happy country", as JRD Tata said, leaders have to think about complete happiness for the people including spiritual happiness, the real goal of a person's life.

▶ Democratic attitude of the king

Apart from "happiness of the people", Chanakya also refers to another aspect of happiness in governance, which is the "democratic attitude" of the king.

Is true democracy only a form of governance or much more? Many countries in the world are still ruled by a king or queen, but their citizens are happy. Their leaders are progressive thinkers and include everyone in their plans and schemes of growth. On the other hand, in some countries that have a democratic form of governance, the citizens are not happy. India, the largest democracy in the world, is an example of this.

The form of governance is the best in the world. We choose our leaders and ruling political party every five years. We have one of the best constitutions in the world. Every single citizen, irrespective of gender, religion, caste, etc., has a right to vote. The law gives a fair hearing to even the most hardened criminal in the courts. Such rights are far from reality in many countries of the world. Yet, people are unhappy.

That is because India lacks only one thing: good leaders.

Even though we elect our leaders, we find that our leaders' "attitude" is not that of great leaders. The ability to think big, take bold decisions, encourage creativity and efficiency and a fighting spirit is what makes a great leader.

Chanakya teaches leaders about their right attitude.

"In the happiness of the subjects lies the happiness of the king." This is real democracy. If the leader understands this, he will make his country happy. But most leaders only think of their own happiness. What makes a leader happy does not necessarily make his people happy. But, what makes the people happy should make him happy.

This is not very difficult to understand, if you put yourself in the shoes of a parent. When a child is crying, the parents do everything they can to help the child. Once the child is out of pain and the smile returns on its face, the parents and other family members are also happy. In the happiness of the child lies the happiness of the parents.

For this attitude to be developed, a leader cannot be selfish. Nor can he impose his ideas as a command or diktat. The leader has to be empathetic, caring and loving. Only then can a leader feel the pain and unhappiness of the citizens and work tirelessly to find solutions to their problems.

In a country where leaders have become dealers, and are thinking of only filling their own pockets, such an attitude cannot be developed.

▶ Self-interest vs subjects' interest

"What is dear to himself is not beneficial to the king," says Chanakya. A leader cannot sit back lazily. He has to step out of his comfort zone and take up difficult tasks, looking at the long-term benefits of his work. These tasks may not benefit him personally, but if his people are benefited, he should take them up, irrespective of his personal likes or dislikes.

"What concerns his subjects is what is beneficial to him," Chanakya adds. In the long term, we realize that the work we did for others actually benefits us.

No action in the world goes without an impact. No good work goes unrecognized. As a leader, you should not expect personal benefits, but the Almighty will give you the due benefits in one form or the other.

Leaders have to understand that no work is big or small. The attitude with which you work is what ultimately matters. In leadership, small beginnings are great beginnings.

So, treat every customer as the most important customer, every citizen as the king, every child as your child and every problem that others face as your problem. You may not be able to solve every problem, but you can make a difference in the way you handled it. If a situation has come to you, it is a message from God that you must contribute. You can create a small ripple that can create a revolution.

Go give it your best shot; make a dent in the universe.

ACCORDING TO CHANAKYA

Qualities of Good Citizens

TO ENSURE SECURITY is the first duty of a leader. The CEO of an organization is responsible for the employees' safety. Therefore, in factories and businesses that require employees round the clock, such as the business process outsourcing (BPO) industry, the law requires the company to ensure its employees' safety. The company has to make sure that an employee reaches the workplace and back home safely. Thus, many companies today provide transport to their staff.

Similarly, companies ensure safety in workplaces like factories, with measures such as posting safety instructions on machines, displaying posters on safety measures in the work area and training workers and managers.

In the same way, every leader has to ensure the safety of the people dependent on him. A country has to ensure safety from both internal and external enemies. The leader has to be very serious about ensuring safety, for if safety is compromised, the king can lose his throne. All public awakenings are stories of citizens not feeling safe.

While ensuring the safety of citizens, the leader should not be worried. Instead, he should be concerned. There is a difference between being worried and being concerned. A worried person sees a problem and a concerned person solves a problem.

If you are aware that there is a safety issue and a security concern, act on it. Do not just sit there doing nothing.

Once the leader has made a clear decision in his mind, a great leap can be taken forward. Take that decision with the help of others who have taken those leaps before you. Consult them. Make your roadmap clear. Decide a goal and stick to it. Do not quit till you achieve your target.

When you as a leader need to ensure the safety of your citizens, work towards achieving that target with care and seriousness. And take care of every person — men, women, children, old persons, young, crippled, mentally challenged, employed and unemployed.

The *Arthashastra* also reiterates that the king must keep his citizens happy and safe. While doing so, Chanakya defines the qualities that keep the subjects safe and secure (Book 6, Chapter 1, Verse 8).

The qualities of a *Janpada* (the citizens/customers) are:

▶ Strong position in center and frontiers

▶ Sustainable in times of distress

▶ Easy to protect

▶ Providing excellent means of livelihood

▶ Capable of bearing taxes and fines

Let us discuss each of these qualities.

▶ Strong position in center and frontiers

There is a very famous story about Chanakya guiding his students about war strategy. Imagine a plate of hot rice. How will you eat it without burning the fingers? If you put your fingers in the center, they will get burnt. Instead, you should start taking a little quantity of rice from the edges of the plate. When you do that, you realize that towards the borders, the rice is not as hot and you can eat it comfortably.

This is an analogy for war strategy. You never attack the center of a kingdom — its capital — directly, because security measures are the most stringent there. It is surrounded by guards because it is the power center and the residence of the king.

Anyone who directly attacks the power center is sure to get killed. Instead, the strategy of attacking the borders first should be used. Thus, slowly and steadily, one can eliminate the less powerful people and reach the center.

Therefore, a defense strategy should ensure that not only is the center secure, but the frontiers have also been strengthened. If the enemy attacks the center directly, the army is ready to defend and fight back.

However, protecting the frontiers is more critical. Infiltration starts from the borders of a country. Different countries have different types of borders, such as mountainous regions, deserts, forest regions or the sea. Chanakya suggests making forts at all these check points.

In the *Arthashastra*, we find descriptions of various types of forts that were built to protect the citizens from enemy attacks. Shivaji Maharaj from Maharashtra, a very successful king who had studied the *Arthashastra*, used these strategies in his warfare plans. In Maharashtra, there are over 400 forts that Shivaji built at strategic locations. This is *Arthashastra* being demonstrated in execution. No wonder that Shivaji's warfare strategies are still a benchmark in military study.

Preventing infiltration helps to guard against enemies who are across the border. These external enemies can be easily identified because a close watch can be kept over those who want to enter one's territory. Chanakya introduced various check posts and passport and visa systems to control external aggression and infiltration.

However, each kingdom also has enemies operating within its borders. These internal enemies could be spies from rival countries who have entered the kingdom through illegal routes and have started destroying the country, or are gathering information to plan a future war.

Internal enemies could also be traitors to the nation who work for enemy countries. Even though they are the kingdom's citizens by nationality, they are funded and supported by the enemy kingdom and work to achieve its objectives.

The leader's war strategy has to consider all these aspects.

In his time, Chanakya created a strong espionage system. This included a women spy network called the *Vishkanya*. This network was comprised of trained and highly intelligent girls and women, who were state employees and gathered information from the enemy camp. This network could create turnaround warfare strategies in the most difficult situations.

Chanakya also created an informer network consisting of eunuchs, beggars, priests, old ladies and community leaders. Information is the key in strategy.

Today, every nation has its own intelligence network and systems. These agencies work round the clock to protect citizens. They work in total secrecy and many undercover agents risk their lives for their jobs. In most cases, even their family members do not know their real profession. Besides these agencies, the police force plays an important role in eliminating internal enemies and anti-social elements, and also gathers information about enemies operating within the nation's borders.

There is also a danger of the same people turning against their country and working for the enemy. Therefore, Chanakya also created a network of counter-spies. Even as every spy kept an eye on enemies and gathered information, each spy was also watched over by others who were gathering information about him.

This may look confusing and may also reflect a lack of trust among your own people. But that is the real job of a leader.

While you should trust people, trust should not be taken for granted. That is because there can be no compromise on national security. The safety of citizens is the utmost priority.

▶ Sustainable in times of distress

Natural calamities such as floods, earthquakes, volcanoes and droughts come without notice and wreak havoc on a nation. A leader has to understand that these have to be accounted for while planning for the welfare of the people. Governments have started creating disaster management groups to handle such calamities.

Special budgets and provisions have to be made and experts should be available to take action immediately. Even these natural calamities have to be tackled on a war footing.

Therefore, Chanakya says a good leader is one who is capable of survival in times of distress.

It may appear difficult to prepare for natural calamities that may or may not occur in the future, but looking at the past trends of natural disasters in the region can help. In a city like Mumbai, waterlogging during the monsoon is quite common. States like Odisha experience floods every year. In Japan, earthquakes are quite common.

By studying these situations, a leader can plan how to handle them when they reoccur. Learn from past mistakes and plan your future strategy.

Sustainability is the key word here. If the leader does not take care of the people during times of distress, they will migrate to other places where they feel safer.

In a globalized era, people can easily migrate to other places and countries. People usually migrate when they have lost faith in the leadership. Even in times of distress, people will not migrate if they have confidence on their leader. This trust in the leader and his abilities in times of distress is the litmus test of leadership.

It is said, "When the going gets tough, the tough get going." That is leadership. In the toughest situations, the leader is able to provide hope.

Even corporate leaders have been able to demonstrate this. When the whole world feels the situation is beyond redemption, the leader walks in and gives the strong message, "Together, we shall win." Such leaders uplift people's spirits and show a way out. They leave a lasting impact for generations to come.

▶ **Easy to protect**

Citizens feel safe when they get protection quickly. Therefore, the systems' response time has to be quick. The leader s hould be very efficient and should be able to protect his people with ease.

Imagine if you dial an emergency number and there is no response on the other end. The first feeling is of insecurity. But, if the phone is answered on the first ring and the person reaches you in a few minutes, you feel safe and reassured.

When a mother is protecting her child, she will make sure the distance between her and the child is as short as possible. Even when she is working in the kitchen, her eyes and ears are on the child. If there is an emergency, she will rush to the child immediately. She will make sure the child is easy to protect.

She is aware of the dangers the child may come across and will try to keep the child away from these. She will ensure there are no harmful objects within the child's reach, the floor is not slippery and emergency medicines are available in the house. She ensures she can contact the doctor at a moment's notice and her social support system, like elders, is always available.

The child may not be aware of all this, but the mother has carefully planned the protection and safety of the child, as she is continuously thinking about the child's welfare.

Even when she is sleeping, the mother is subconsciously alert and vigilant about the child.

When there is a problem, she is completely ready to tackle it. Come what may, she never forgets the fact that the safety and security of the child is her first and foremost priority. For this, she ensures the child should be easy to protect.

Leaders have to be to their citizens what these mothers are to their children.

▶ Providing excellent means of livelihood

To ensure employment to everyone is a major key result area (KRA) of any leader or government. Human beings and society have a deep relationship with economics. Money is important in the daily transactions of our lives.

Therefore, a good leader has to make sure everyone in his kingdom has excellent means of livelihood. Note here, that Chanakya refers not just to money required for basic survival but "excellent" means of livelihood, meaning enough money to ensure a quality life.

Quality life comes from ensuring that a person earns more money than is required to meet expenses.

In India especially, the family is culturally an important part of an individual's life. We are trained to take care of our siblings, children and parents. We are also told to contribute to society and social causes.

All of that requires money. The leader has to understand this fact, and ensure that a person can earn more than what he needs to spend. Regular cash flow to a person, family or organization ensures financial freedom and security. It should also be followed by good insurance and investment plans. Saving for the rainy day is important during the sunny days.

A good and steady income instills confidence in every person. To pay good salaries is also the quality of great leadership. In many successful companies, the employees are paid very well. Nations that pay their scientists, teachers, thinkers, artists, policemen and armed forces well have good quality of life.

Thus, for the citizens to be happy, financial planning is important for the leader and should not be neglected.

▶ Capable of bearing taxes and fines

Taxes and fines are revenue for the government. The money thus collected is used for paying salaries of government employees, defence, education, health care, development of infrastructure and other projects that are important for social and national growth.

Therefore, it is the citizen's duty to pay taxes on time. In the *Arthashastra*, Chanakya says that "The person who does not pay taxes brings to himself the sins of the king." It is considered a sinful act not to pay taxes.

However, Chanakya has a balanced approach. He says that taxes and fines should be imposed only to the extent of people's capability to pay.

This policy ensures a win-win situation. The government gets revenue from the people, while the citizens are happy to pay as much as they are capable of paying.

Such a society is a happy society.

PART C

LEADERSHIP IN ACTION

Taking Care of Citizens

The safety and happiness of society are the objects at which all political institutions aim, and to which all such institutions must be sacrificed.

JAMES MADISON, 4ᵀᴴ US PRESIDENT

THE POLICE PLAY a major role in taking care of a country's citizens.

A good policing system ensures peace and progress in society. The police are the tough hand of the government. They deal with sections of society that most people do not like to face. A policeman comes across murders, rapes and accidents daily in the course of his work.

On the other hand, policemen also meet people from various walks of life, such as politicians, businessmen, artists, celebrities and also the common man. They have to eliminate the evil and protect the good. This is a job with multiple dimensions. They practice Chanakya's principles in reality, applying the theory of *Sama, Dana, Danda* and *Bheda* in providing protection to citizens.

Sama is using the method of discussion and guidance. If you ever observe a policeman in a police station, you will find that he often plays the role of a counselor. For instance, when two people have a fight and land up at a police station, the police are trained to calm them down and give valuable advice, which would solve the problem immediately.

In a nation like India, where court cases can last for years, the police offer valuable suggestions to solve the problem in a peaceful manner, rather than taking the legal route which is time-consuming, irritating and costly.

Dana means explaining the benefits. The police explain the benefits of sorting out problems in a peaceful manner. Peaceful solutions have many advantages over long-lasting, dirty fights that can continue for several generations. Understanding the benefits sometimes makes a person rethink and take a different course of action.

Peace is the route which has multiple benefits. The policeman ensures the message is given at the right time, not after the quarreling parties have lost time and energy.

Danda means showing the rod or being strict. A policeperson knows when to use the rod and has been empowered to do so. Chanakya calls this "*Danda-niti*". This is another method of controlling anti-social elements in a society, which has been widely explained in the *Arthashastra*.

The rod is a symbol of power and also fear. The message is that wrongdoers cannot take things for granted. If a person crosses the limits set by law or society, the policeman uses the rod to restore discipline.

Bheda means elimination. When the good ways do not work, the tough decision to eliminate the wrongdoer has to be taken. Showing the rod is different from using the gun. If a gangster or terrorist is attacking a crowd, the police have no choice but to use the power given to them — the license to kill.

Police operations are required when situations get out of control. If a limb is infected, doctors will often advise amputation in order to save the whole body. Similarly, when no other method works, some people who are harmful to the country have to be eliminated.

In taking care of citizens, Sivanandhan also proved how Chanakya's principles could be put into practice. Let us see how this was done.

▶ Strong position in center and frontiers

Sivanandhan describes his role as a leader taking care of citizens, "I was very clear that after gaining the confidence of my own people, I needed to connect with my citizens. Being connected to the common man was my role." During his tenure, wherever he was posted, he always tried to connect with the common man.

Thus, he was clear that his mental positioning was strong – being with the people and protecting them from internal (central) enemies and external (frontiers) enemies. We see this in the police force preparing to defend the country against any future terror attacks.

Sivanandhan also believed in empowering people to take care of their own security. During his tenure, he realized that in many cases, the common man could be trained in certain skills that are known only to the police force, so that they can play the police role themselves. "Give a man a fish and you feed him for a day. Teach a man to fish and you feed him for a lifetime," is a popular proverb. This is how you empower people.

For example, the Indian Hotel and Restaurant Association (AHAR) came to the Mumbai police with complaints of receiving threatening calls. On Sivanandhan's behest, representatives of the Association were given gun licenses and technical training on how to record phone calls. They were able to use this knowledge to nab the wrongdoers threatening them.

Thus, the skill of recording calls was transferred to the concerned people and their dependence on the police was reduced. They were now empowered to "fish for a lifetime".

▶ Sustainable in times of distress

Sivanandhan was available at the time of any distress or emergency. And quick action ensured a feeling of confidence in people. The capacity to handle emergencies was built through various methods.

He explains, "My mobile number was freely given to everyone. It was announced in the papers and through the media. There was no hierarchy that restricted a common man from meeting me. Anyone could write an email to me directly. Decisions were taken quickly and delegated to the right person to ensure fast results."

Sivanandhan connected to various groups of society through various methods. He took various initiatives to reach out to the youth, children, women and senior citizens.

One way of doing this was through websites. Some of the websites he started are: *www.copconnect.in*, *www.hamarisuraksha.com*, *www.nagpurpolice.org*, *www.thanepolice.org* and *www.mumbaipolice.org*

All these were interactive websites where the citizens could connect with Sivanandhan and the police force. Thus, the communication gap between the common man and the police was reduced.

▶ Easy to protect

By making the police more accessible to the common man, Sivanandhan also ensured that the citizens were easy to protect.

People require constant communication and confidence building measures. When you do that, citizens connect with you and feel you are there to protect them. These measures look small in the beginning, but have a huge impact.

The role of media in confidence building measures cannot be denied.

Sivanandhan says, "I would like to thank the media who helped me take these messages to many people in a big way. The power of the media, if it works hand in hand (with the police), can work wonders."

During his career, Sivanandhan did various television interviews, radio shows, meetings with newspaper journalists and webcasts. Speaking sessions at Rotary and Lions clubs and at colleges and schools were ways to reach everyone.

He also followed an open-door policy in office to make himself accessible to everyone. This had a huge impact.

His aim was to bring about a positive change in the image of the police. So far, the criminals would take the police for granted and the common man kept his distance. He wanted gangsters and criminals to fear and the common man to start trusting the police.

Sivanandhan explains that the police are always on the side of the common man. They are helpers and enablers of the good. It is due to the wrong actions of a few policemen that this image has been tarnished. But the greatest motivation for a policeman is respect and appreciation from the common man. Sometimes, a small positive mention in the newspapers about police action towards protecting the common masses will go a long way in boosting the police morale.

Another initiative that Sivanandhan took was to connect with the youth. Youth represents the energy and hope of a nation. If the youth of our country can be given the right values and direction, we will be a transformed nation.

Since film stars have a huge impact on the youth of our nation, Sivanandhan worked closely with these stars to connect with the youth. A short film with Shahrukh Khan to connect to the cops was made.

This was also the time when the number of deaths of senior citizens living alone in Mumbai was on the rise. To tackle the problems faced by this vulnerable group of people, who are dependent on their children and other support systems, Sivanandhan took the initiative to launch a helpline number (103) for emergencies for senior citizens, women and children. He also launched a website — *www.hamarisuraksha.com* — to help the Mumbai police and NGOs manage the safety and security of senior citizens. He got Simi Garewal, the film actor, to inaugurate the site at the Malabar Hill Club.

Post the Mumbai terror attack of 26/11, many initiatives were taken to tighten security and be better prepared for such attacks. But having taken these initiatives was not enough; Sivanandhan wanted the common man to understand that the police were better prepared now, in order to instill a sense of security in the common man. For this, on November 26, 2009, the first anniversary of the 26/11 terrorist Mumbai attacks, he organized a parade from the Oberoi Trident to Girgaum Chowpatty to showcase these police initiatives to the common man. It was demonstrated to the citizens that the police was ready with superior equipment and well-trained policemen. "Your safety is our responsibility" was the message that was sent to all.

Sivanandhan thus ensured that citizens' protection was the topmost priority of the police force.

He also started professional magazines like *Protector* and *Samvaad*, to spread awareness. These magazines describe the internal functioning and work of the police force.

Even at a personal level, Sivanandhan was very empathetic towards citizens. To quote an example, he once paid for the rehabilitation of a girl who was the victim of an acid attack.

Bhivandi children's remand home

The concept of corporate social responsibility (CSR) is very popular today. But more important than CSR is personal social responsibility or PSR. As a police leader, apart from taking decisions for the police force, Sivanandhan also needed to show his personal commitment towards society's well-being.

Here is another case where he went beyond the role of a police cop to help the citizens. This was the transformation of the children's remand home at Bhivandi. Sivanandhan felt that these children needed a protected environment and affection. So, he sought the involvement of consulting firm, Deloitte through their CSR initiative, IMPACT Day. Thus, the remand home was given a makeover, with freshly painted walls and refurbished interiors, along with upgrades in facilities. Sivanandhan contributed money and also got involved in making the remand home an ISO 9001 organization. Besides, he adopted one of the inmates, a speech and hearing impaired girl, and paid for her treatment, medical expenses and special education.

During Sivanandhan's term as Commissioner of Police, the children's remand home in Bhivandi, in Thane district, was much transformed.

Sneha Joshi, who works for the remand home, said, "By chance, one day, Sivanandhan sir visited our center. The only responsibility he had as a policeman was to ensure police protection is given to these children. When he started speaking to the children, he came across Mamata who had a disability – she could not speak or listen. He was so touched that from that day onwards, he took complete responsibility for her treatment, education and other requirements. He took care of her as (if she were) his own daughter."

The remand center changed completely under Sivanandhan's leadership. He raised funds for them. The drawing and greeting cards made by the children were put on exhibition and sale. Medicines and other requirements were supplied. He also created a home theater for the remand home as children could not go out much to public places for entertainment. He organized games for them, distributed prizes and would spend a full day with them on a yearly basis. Yoga sessions and counseling were organized so that once out of the remand home, these children could have a bright future.

Some of these children could go on to become future die-hard criminals. Sivanandhan deeply felt the need to make sure that the society that had so far neglected these children, should take good care of them once they were out.

A society which invests in the future of orphans and abandoned children will definitely create a paradise on earth.

▶ Providing excellent means of livelihood

About his working style, Sivanandhan says, "I believed in the least amount of paperwork and my table was always clear. In a government organization, pending files means decision-making is pending. The common man should never be affected by pending paperwork."

As a police leader, it was important for Sivanandhan to pay people in time. It could be the policemen and policewomen whose salaries had to be paid in time (so that they can earn their livelihood), or it could be clearing some vendor's payment. Through good administrative skills, efficient paperwork and good decision making, he ensured that everyone got their dues cleared on time.

▶ Capable of bearing taxes and fines

Taxes and fines are sources of revenue for the government. But for people to pay their taxes, businesses have to flourish. A safe environment has to be created for business activities to take place. It was after Sivanandhan and his team broke the underworld's control over Mumbai that businessmen regained confidence in the government.

Sivanandhan was instrumental in the resurgence of economic activity in the city, thus ensuring good collection of taxes and fines for the government.

★ TIPS TO KEEP CITIZENS HAPPY ★

1. Connect with people: If they do not come to you, you should go to them.

2. Use the power of the media: It is a great partner for doing good work.

3. Show what you have done: Your customers/citizens should know about the initiatives you have taken for their security and happiness.

4. Follow an open-door policy: You should be accessible to everyone.

5. Empower customers/citizens: Impart training on your skills.

The Leader in Me

Notes

Chapter 4

Durg

FORT/INFRASTRUCTURE

Swami	the king
Amatya	the minister
Janpada	the country
Durg	**the fortified city**
Kosha	the treasury
Dand	the army
Mitra	the ally

PART A

THE FOURTH SECRET

Durg: Infrastructure

IN ANCIENT TIMES, the *durg* or fort had many uses. Forts were located at strategic points, such as mountaintops or the coast, and helped the king to keep a lookout for enemies. There were small and large forts, depending on the location and the purpose for which they were built.

Some forts were big, fortified cities. A complete civilization lived inside such a *durg*. The high boundary walls protected the citizens inside the fort from external threats.

All kinds of people stayed inside the fort, from the king and his ministers to the citizens of the kingdom. It was like the capital of a kingdom and those who visited this fortified city had to take special permission to get inside. It was like getting a visa before entering a new country.

The fortified city had various facilities, such as water tanks, roads, well-built houses, stores for foodgrains, drainage systems, a marketplace and more. Temples, places for recreation, gardens and playgrounds were built inside the *durg* based on systems of Vaastu.

That is the reason why Chanakya has suggested the *durg* to be an important pillar of a kingdom. The *durg* protects the citizens and also gives them ample scope for development. Some historians consider the study of forts very important to understand the development of a civilization.

Architects of today also study them to understand the town planning that existed in the past.

One of the most important lessons to be drawn from fort infrastructure is to plan for best- and worst-case scenarios and be well-prepared for any situation. Both human and natural factors must be considered while planning infrastructure.

In Book 8, Chapter 1, Verse 2 of the *Arthashastra*, Chanakya says,

"A calamity of a constituent, of a divine or human origin, springs from ill luck or wrong policy."

During a workshop for a group of managers, the participants were asked, "Assume there is a fire in this hotel, and in spite of the fire protection systems, about 50 people die. Who will be held responsible?"

There were two sets of answers. The first group said, "The hotel management would be responsible, for they did not have enough fire-protection measures. Fire-exit routes were not per norms or may not have been updated."

The second set said, "It is bad luck. Despite a strong fire-safety policy, 50 people could not escape the fire."

That is exactly what Chanakya says too. Any disaster is due to ill luck or wrong policy.

Let us look at what ill luck means. In life, irrespective of how much you plan, things can go wrong. Human beings may have done their best and installed world-class systems. Yet, an unknown, unforeseen factor can ruin the whole plan.

An example of this is satellite launches or missile testing. Years of research and billions of rupees are spent on the development. Thousands of scientists work round the clock to make the perfect launch. Yet, when the missile or satellite takes off, no one is sure if it will succeed.

If it succeeds, everybody is happy. But if it fails, who can be blamed? It is called bad luck. The team tries to learn from its mistakes and returns to the drawing board.

There are many instances in every person's life where even the best efforts can come to naught at the last moment. A sports team that practiced the whole year may lose the final match to an easy opponent. A doctor may lose a patient in the operation theatre, even though he has the best experience in the world. It is bad luck.

However, one cannot just blame bad luck without proper planning and efforts. One cannot go to an examination hall without preparation. One has to work very hard and give more than 100 percent. If we study the lives of successful people, we will find that be it an Olympic medal winner, a successful businessman or a police officer, all of them have spent sleepless nights preparing for success.

If one accepts a challenge and does not prepare for it, and then blames others for the failure, it is not a sign of good leadership. It is wrong policy, since there was no planning or execution.

As leaders, we need to understand that right policies are about lots of planning and effort.

One cannot wait for surprises. One has to prepare for surprises well in advance. And for that, we need to be very vigilant and alert to unknown possibilities.

Calamities or disasters are of two types: divine or of human origin. Natural calamities like floods, earthquakes, storms and droughts are of divine nature. Man may have less control over them, yet he can learn from history and plan for these natural calamities.

Disasters of human origin include terrorism and mass murders by leaders of nations. These can be avoided by careful planning.

For example, after the fire in the Mantralaya of Maharashtra on June 21, 2012, which demonstrated how ill-prepared the building was for such a disaster, the Brihanmumbai Municipal Corporation (BMC) has started taking measures to prevent such problems in future. Surprise inspections of various societies in the city for fire safety are being conducted and necessary action is being taken against societies that have violated fire-safety regulations.

In a city like Mumbai, earthquakes are not very common, yet the government authorities ensure that all new constructions are earthquake-proof, have adequate water supply and plan for the worst situations. There are many districts in Maharashtra where droughts are common. Planning for water becomes an important part of disaster management in those districts.

Policemen tackle both human and natural disasters. In each region, the police force and supplies are planned after considering the history of human and natural disasters in that region. In places that have a history of communal riots, taking measures for communal harmony is part of planning. In areas with inadequate rainfall, water shortage can create a law and order problem. The police plans in a different manner for these areas.

Therefore, a leader is advised to plan infrastructure in such a manner that both man-made and natural disasters are prevented.

What is a *durg* in the business world?

Businessmen also require good infrastructure to run their businesses successfully. The definition of the *durg* changes according to the nature of the business. The head office of a business, from where the CEO or chairman operates, can be called its control tower.

If the business is in the manufacturing segment, the factory, including the plant, machinery and other equipment, becomes part of the infrastructure. A carefully constructed factory that takes safety and hygiene into account and complies with international benchmarks puts the company on a global platform.

Expand the concept of the *durg* in the case of a modern nation. Good roads, flyovers, bridges, houses are all important for nation building. In the eleventh five-year plan of India, 9% of the gross domestic product (GDP) has been allocated to infrastructure development. The twelfth five-year plan also includes infrastructure development as a major component of the national budget.

In the case of the police, infrastructure includes the police stations, weapons, vehicles and more. In the case study of this chapter, you will read more about how changes in infrastructure created a productive and positive work atmosphere for the police force.

In today's world, infrastructure is not just physical, but also digital. Apart from having good offices, digital infrastructure which includes computers, the internet and mobile phones is equally important. This is more so because of the growing trend of working from home and telecommuting. And infrastructure all over — in airports, coffee shops, hotels, restaurants, even inside buses — is enabling this trend. Therefore, when you invest in digital infrastructure, you should ensure that it is supportive of telecommuting for those employees who may require it.

As a leader, it is important to ensure world-class infrastructure for your organization. Move with the times and get the best that is available. Remember that technology is a very important enabler in today's digitally connected world and invest in the best that is available to meet your needs.

If you do not build your *durg* well, your team will be demotivated. Gone are the days when people stuck to an organization for a lifetime. The opportunities are vast and the choices are many. So, creating good working conditions is essential for any organization that wants to retain employees.

I know of people who have left companies because of bad toilets. Similarly, having good chairs, proper ventilation, aesthetically pleasing decor, good lighting and canteen facilities are necessary. Even security measures like CCTVs and fire exits are important for leaders who want to build great organizations.

In the police, Sivanandhan worked on "transforming" the workplace. Some of the experiments that he conducted in the workplace have become benchmarks for other police officers.

Sivanandhan believes that leadership is also about setting a trend, a standard that others will love to duplicate. Today, when he looks back at his career and when young IPS officers come to him for guidance and discussions, he is happy to see that the next generation wants to make things better and take the benchmark forward.

PART B

ACCORDING TO CHANAKYA

Qualities of Good Infrastructure

TO BUILD GOOD infrastructure, you first need to create the blueprint or master plan. If you get this right, building the infrastructure becomes easy. In many cases, you may have a good plan, but as you keep working on the details and people give you inputs, the plan keeps evolving and changing. The more you plan in detail in the initial stages, the better it will be towards the end.

When Sivanandhan started building the infrastructure of his department, he considered everything his force may want, such as good housing, schooling or health facilities. When you consider different perspectives in creating your blueprint, more people benefit from the infrastructure that you build. Infrastructure has to be "built to last."

As a leader, when you have to build a good office, there could be two situations.

The first could be that you need to build the infrastructure from scratch. This is called a green field project.

A green field project is relatively easy because it is like starting on a plain canvas. You can draw any picture you want. There are unlimited choices; the only limitations are your imagination and the budget. For instance, if a person has been given a piece of land to construct housing facilities for the police force, the look of the final structure will be based on innovation and creativity.

It can be built like an existing police quarters; it can be designed like the better-looking police quarters in another country; it can even be a totally unique structure that sets a standard in building police quarters.

The second situation is when you have to renovate an existing infrastructure. This is called a brown field project, where you have to take up an existing, functional infrastructure, and create a new project in the same place with minimal disruptions to the existing infrastructure.

The challenges are very different in this case. Let us take the example of 50-year-old police quarters, where people are staying and have facilities such as schools, markets and hospitals. This structure needs to be pulled down and rebuilt, because the planning of five decades ago is insufficient for present needs, the foundations of buildings have weakened and buildings themselves are dilapidated.

The project leader has to plan the infrastructure considering present needs. He also has to consider factors such as alternative accommodation for the residents when the buildings are pulled down; the schooling of their children at the alternative accommodation; rules and regulations in creating the new infrastructure; convincing residents about the necessity of redevelopment and handling any resistance towards paying higher maintenance charges, when the residents move into the new buildings.

That is why, in a city like Mumbai, slum redevelopment is taking more time than was originally planned. The leader has to listen to the opinions of the people while building the plan. At times, redevelopment will have to be done in phases, without disrupting the existing system.

Think like a designer and architect while creating new infrastructure. Ask these questions:

▶ What kind of look do I want?

▶ What will people feel about it?

▶ Have I considered the inputs of others?

▶ Am I thinking long term while building it?

▶ How will I manage the budget?

▶ Will people resist the change?

▶ What approvals are required?

▶ How soon can I make it?

Think on paper. Write down the problems and their alternative solutions. Then, think through various possibilities to tackle each problem. Take suggestions from others; think out of the box; think laterally. By thus applying your mind, you will be able to develop the best infrastructure.

In this chapter, you will also read the story of building the Thane Police School — an infrastructure that never existed, but has now inspired many other senior police officers.

But, before we do that, let us take Chanakya's inputs on building infrastructure.

In Book 6, Chapter 1, Verse 8 of the *Arthashastra*, he says that the *durg* should have the following qualities:

▶ Aesthetically pleasing

▶ Beneficial to men

At the same time, people, who are also part of the infrastructure of an organization or country, should have the following qualities:

▶ Dedication to work

▶ Loyalty and honesty

These are eternal qualities of good infrastructure. Chanakya has listed many more qualities, but we will discuss these four aspects for our purpose. The first two qualities pertain to "hard infrastructure", meaning what people can see and feel. The remaining two pertain to "soft infrastructure", that is, people's attitude while working in an organization.

The leader takes the first two qualities into consideration while creating the physical infrastructure. But the next two qualities have to be developed by the people themselves. Of course, the leader plays a major role in inspiring his people to develop these qualities. As we have seen in previous chapters, an inspired leader can create an inspiring work culture.

▶ Aesthetically pleasing

Any infrastructure you build must be pleasing and peaceful. It should look beautiful and impart a sense of well-being to visitors as well as those who work there. Recall how you feel in a five-star hotel — the well-designed, well-maintained surroundings and courteous staff make you feel welcome and cared for. That is the aim of good infrastructure.

Besides being beautiful, the infrastructure must also be functional. Visitors should not feel lost or unwelcome. The staff should be polite and should help the visitor achieve the purpose of his or her visit. This was one of Sivanandhan's achievements when he was in charge of immigration (1987-91). As mentioned earlier, he succeeded in transforming the office into a positive workplace with a corporate feel and an attitude of seriousness towards solving the problems of citizens and visitors. With that, he achieved one of the greatest breakthroughs in the police department.

Spend on making the infrastructure look good. Select the right colors, use good material and classy designs. Today, with mass manufacturing, you can get good quality at economical prices. Do some reading and research, visit websites, ask designers and check the varieties available in the market.

The result of your efforts will be infrastructure that is good to look at, and makes both your workers and visitors happy.

▶ **Beneficial to men**

In building infrastructure, the needs of the people who will use it should be considered. If you involve these people and understand their problems, the infrastructure can be built to offer solutions to those problems.

For example, the report of an employee survey at a multinational software company showed low energy and high levels of fatigue in employees. It was revealed that to boost their energy levels and reduce fatigue, employees would like to eat food at short intervals during the day.

However, the canteen was far away from the work areas. People waited for lunch breaks, because of the distance and time taken to travel to the canteen. This had affected employee productivity to a large extent.

Once the company understood this problem, new infrastructure was created to solve it. Refrigerators and food shelves were bought and loaded with energy drinks and nutritious food. These were placed all over the office such that no employee had to walk more than 20 steps to reach a food point. Employees could have unlimited food during the day, free of cost.

The result of this initiative was increased energy levels, productivity and efficiency of the employees.

Here is another example. When Sivanandhan was a Commissioner of Police at Thane, he would often observe cops having tea at a roadside stall. He decided to build a restaurant in the area, where the policepersons could chat with their colleagues and have light snacks as well. That is how Urjita Restaurant & Lunch Home came into being.

This is as important for a policeman as it is for a software engineer. After all, policemen too work and think hard through the day. And unlike software engineers who have desk jobs, policemen face harsh physical conditions and high levels of air and noise pollution in the course of their work.

Thus, a leader should ensure the workplace is inspiring to him as well as to his subordinates and employees. Since people today spend most of their time in their workplaces, the workplace infrastructure should make them feel at home.

▶ Dedication to work

Building good physical infrastructure is the first step. The next step is to employ people who are dedicated to work.

People who are corrupt, greedy or selfish will make use of the workplace infrastructure for their personal interests. You find this in various powerful offices, where even though the employees are public servants, they make the public serve them.

The people who work in your organization should be value based. This again begins with the leader who is devoted to the organization's cause. If he uses his power of office for the right reasons, his subordinates will not be able to misuse their power.

If a good man is put into a bad system, he may get corrupted himself. But, if the leader is incorruptible, even a corrupt man in the system will not be able to function. That is the importance of an ethical leader.

Moreover, people in the organization should be able to connect to the leader's vision and dream.

For example, a company was functioning in a small space for over 20 years. Finally, after years of hard work, the leader was able to achieve his dream of constructing a new and bigger office.

When it was inaugurated, the peon remarked, "For the last 20 years, it was my dream too, to have a new office for our company."

This is a man devoted to his work. The peon did not dream of a large salary. He had grown with the organization and had begun to associate with the leader's dream. The peon became more interested in the company's success than in personal success. If a leader can achieve this — to make his dream the dream of his subordinates — he has proved his leadership qualities.

Every person in that organization then gets inspired to work for a higher purpose. Devotion is a state of mind where you dedicate your work to a larger goal, to the welfare of the organization and the society at large.

▶ **Loyalty and honesty**

Despite the fact that they are being paid good salaries and perks, employees in organizations sometimes engage in petty behavior, such as stealing mouse pads or office equipment. This becomes difficult to change.

To earn the loyalty of an organization's employees is an important part of the role a good leader plays in the company. People who keep changing jobs every now and then find it difficult to convince recruiting companies of their competence or loyalty.

The benefits of loyalty can only be seen in the long run. If you work hard and with sincerity, the rewards will come.

Honesty of intent and purpose should be developed in the people. This core value can be easily developed in various corporations and also in the police force, the army or paramilitary force, if the leader, the commissioner of police or the commander of the army himself is a role model.

Such loyalty can be easily built when the leader stands with his team like a friend, philosopher and guide during crises.

Thus, creating a good infrastructure around and inside people builds great organizations.

LEADERSHIP IN ACTION

Building Good Infrastructure

As a nation, a society, a family and an individual, we must be
be grateful to our great ancestors who dedicated their lives to laying
the infrastructure of our livelihood today. Let us continue their path
and build upon it.

MASTER JIN KWON

IN THIS CASE study, you will find out more about the initiatives taken by Sivanandhan to build good infrastructure in his various postings.

Sivanandhan was made the Commissioner of Police of Mumbai in June 2009, soon after the terror attacks on Mumbai on November 26, 2008.

This was the time when the world was looking at Mumbai and India after the terror attack. There was widespread public outrage within the country over the way the terror attack had been handled. National security and the competence of the police had come under scrutiny, both nationally and internationally. The common man had already lost confidence in the government. Various groups came out openly on the streets of Mumbai and across the nation to raise their voice against the system. As a result of this, the Chief Minister and the Home Minister of Maharashtra had to resign.

In the final stages of Sivanandhan's career, there was a task to complete. With limited time in hand, upset and dissatisfied citizens and a government clueless on action steps, all eyes were on him as he took over.

A media person asked him about his priorities. He was clear, "Only one agenda: tackle terrorism."

As a leader, one is responsible for everything. But one needs to understand the current situation and focus on the key problem. This does not mean you ignore the other problems. You are aware of all problems; yet your focus must be on the "key" problem.

It is the 80-20 theory: 80% of your energies should be spent on the key issue, while the remaining 20% can be spent on other issues. For Sivanandhan, 80% of his energies were to be focused on tackling terrorism, while 20% would be on problems such as housing, promotions and salaries for the police force. Leadership is about balancing between multitasking and focus.

During the 1990s, when he broke the underworld nexus, the scenario was different. He could not duplicate what he had done in the past. After 20 years, terrorism had become a global problem with global operations. Yet, there were some similarities between tackling the underworld domination of the 1990s and the aftermath of the terror attacks of 2008. Sivanandhan had to build the confidence of the public, get government approvals as fast as possible, and most important, build the morale of the police force.

When the problem starts with a nation like Pakistan, it does not have an easy solution. Ever since 1947, both nations have fought wars (in 1947, 1965, 1971 and 1999) and also tried to find peaceful solutions.

They have tried to solve their problems through diplomatic meetings of heads of both nations at various times; even economic solutions have been worked out. Cultural programs, exchange programs of artists and musicians and friendly cricket tournaments have been organized in both nations. Various confidence building measures have been taken. Yet, there does not seem to be a permanent solution to this cancerous disease.

At the same time, organizations including the police, army, navy, air force, Border Security Force and Indian Coast Guard cannot take the peace route. They have to be prepared for the worst, a war situation.

26/11 taught the Mumbai police a valuable lesson. Even though they were supposed to take care of law and order within a geographical region with limited resources, they had to be ready for a low-cost "war".

Usually, this role is played by the army and other agencies that have adequate resources and training. From day one, they have been trained to kill the enemy on the border, while the police force is trained to tackle criminals, manage traffic, take care of senior citizens and investigate robberies and murders. All this is very different from being trained to handle a national war.

But, as a leader, Sivanandhan decided not to sit back and blame the government saying, "This was not my job," or "Without enough bullet-proof jackets and arms and ammunition, how do you expect us to fight a war which is usually fought by the army?"

Instead, he decided that the time for change had come.

The Maharashtra police would now evolve into a national force as strong as the army; it would become the benchmark in policing. He made his plans very clear to the government. What was never done in the past, needed to be done today to tackle the problems of the future.

He had to change the image of the police, give it a complete makeover.

The following measures were taken for the first time in the history of the Maharashtra police:

▸ ₹ 126 crore was sanctioned by the government based on various proposals sent.

▸ Several speed boats were bought. The police began working closely with the Indian Coast Guard, as the terrorists had come through the sea route.

▸ 1,500 MP3 and MP4 guns and ammunition were purchased.

▸ 40 Marksman bullet-proof jeeps and several small combat vehicles were purchased.

▸ Five simulators were purchased, so that policemen would be able to practice firing in urban and rural settings. The RD Pradhan Committee report had pointed out that the police force did not have sufficient ammunition for firing practice. The procurement of simulators eased this constraint.

▸ Various new institutions came into being, such as Force 1, in line with the NSG commandos, and the Quick Response Team (QRT) consisting of 1,500 policemen. World-class training sessions were organized for policemen. For instance, the QRT was trained by top commandos.

The next step was to make the common man aware of the measures taken, so that he could feel safe.

For this, apart from creating a force that was equipped for a war-like situation, Sivanandhan constantly communicated with the citizens of the country about the steps the police force had taken.

These were the measures taken for communication:

▸ Utilizing the media: The media helped to convey the message about the measures taken, not only locally or nationally, but also internationally.

▸ Participating in lecture tours: Sivanandhan personally addressed various clubs, community gatherings, schools and colleges, asking people not to be afraid. The professor in him was coming alive. The key message given was, "We are responsible for your safety."

▶ Organizing seminars: He invited some of the key strategy experts to share their inputs on national security. These included APJ Abdul Kalam, MK Narayanan, Julio Rebeiro, Ajay Sahney, Anil Kakodkar, R Mashelkar, Shyamal Datta, MJ Akbar, Sundeep Waslekar and KPS Gill. Sivanandhan's objective was to encourage the police force to interact with global experts and gain exposure to new ideas and feel encouraged and optimistic, rather than retreating into a shell after the demoralizing experience of 26/11.

▶ Organizing a memorial parade: On the first anniversary of 26/11, in 2009, the parade was taken from the Oberoi Trident hotel to Girgaum Chowpatty. The aim of the parade was to showcase the new equipment purchased and the training given. This was almost like a Republic Day parade, where the strength of a nation is showcased.

▶ Imparting information in police stations: Posters regarding the new equipment, training and security measures were created and put up in police stations, as a confidence-building measure for the police force.

Even though the post of DGP was the final post in Sivanandhan's career, where most of his energies and resources were used to build world-class police infrastructure, building such lasting infrastructure was always part of Sivanandhan's style of leadership. Leaders should understand that infrastructure is beyond just beautiful interiors. It is a message you send to others that we are determined to be world-class. We are serious about our business. And most important, we care about you.

Here is a look at some of the infrastructure Sivanandhan built through his career. You will see that the qualities of good infrastructure described by Chanakya can be seen in reality here.

▶ **Aesthetically pleasing**

Gymnasiums: Even in the police force, Sivanandhan prioritized the health of his people. He created 25 world-class gymnasiums with the best available equipment in the police stations. After the infrastructure of the gymnasiums was improved, more and more policemen and policewomen began using them.

Sivanandhan created gymnasiums that were aesthetically pleasing and housed world-class equipment. Everyone felt a sense of pride when they used these gymnasiums.

▶ **Beneficial to men**

Besides building world-class hospitals and training centers, Sivanandhan also brought about significant improvements to infrastructure in police stations. All of this infrastructure is beneficial to the police force.

Hospitals: Hospitals are not just places where you find doctors and nurses. It is a place of hope for everyone. When one comes to a hospital, there are mixed feelings of fear and hope. A good, clean hospital with caring doctors goes a long way in reassuring patients and their families and making them feel more confident about recovery. The icing on the cake is when the hospital expenses are also taken care of. Sivanandhan worked on a system for building hospitals and health care centers.

His priority was to build a state-of-the-art hospital that would provide facilities at economical rates to policepersons, as the existing hospital was old and dilapidated. Sivanandhan undertook to build a massive sports stadium at the cost ₹ 2.5 crore, in which he accommodated an ATM of the State Bank of India, a provisions store for police families and a hospital with seven air-conditioned rooms for super-specialty doctors from

Wockhardt hospital, with whom a 10-year MoU has been signed. Many corporate houses have donated a variety of expensive equipment, including a dental chair, a color Doppler machine, instruments for the Opthalmology department and a fully-equipped ambulance.

Thanks to Sivanandhan's vision, 7,000 policemen and their families, who were hitherto neglected in the government-owned civil hospital, could accrue immediate benefits.

Sivanandhan was also instrumental in creating a health reference manual for the police force. Forty thousand copies were printed and distributed to each person in the force. Health checkups of all men were done regularly and health problems were tackled on a case-to-case basis.

Yoga classes, sports events and tips on diet and nutrition were also created and organized with the help of experts. The aim was to improve the health of the police force.

Thus, Sivanandhan ensured that the health of his force was taken care of.

Creating hospitals, gyms and nursing homes is creating hard infrastructure. But, creating an environment of health and safety is soft infrastructure.

Police station improvements: The police station is like a charging point for the police force. Like a mobile phone which needs to be charged at an electric point from time to time, the police station is the place where the cops come to work hard, but also to rejuvenate and refresh between bouts of hectic activity. As mentioned earlier, unlike a corporate job which could be limited to the four walls of the office, the policeman is continuously on the move. The police station is where he comes for a short break amidst his long and tiring day.

Sivanandhan worked hard to make the police station a place where cops could get re-energized. With the increasing number of policewomen in the force, providing special facilities to women and building women-friendly infrastructure was important. Toilets, restrooms and places to have food and chat with colleagues were created.

The cops were eating and drinking at roadside shanties. Therefore, a police café was built inside the CP office. The policemen's wives were trained by Padmashri Prema Purav; these ladies ran the police café and enjoyed the profits. The entire capital expenditure for the café was borne by the Maharashtra Chamber of Housing Industry (MCHI).

The need for a restaurant in the police quarters was expressed. So, a restaurant called Urjita was built and given on rent to a local restaurateur. This yielded monthly profits towards the Police Welfare Fund.

Even the administration side of the police station was upgraded with good computers, user-friendly technology and specific software designed for police-related work. With the help of the National Association of Software and Services Companies (NASSCOM), a state-of-the-art cyber-crime lab was created in the CP office at the cost of ₹ 75 lakh. So far, 2,600 policemen from all over the state have been trained in cyber-crime detection and investigation. Management Information Systems (MIS) were also upgraded for faster and more efficient performance.

Training Centers: The growth of any institution depends on the quality of training it imparts to its people. The policemen also need training on a regular basis. The entry-level training imparted during induction gets outdated with time.

To make the police force efficient and effective, it is important to upgrade technical knowledge, and develop hard and soft skills.

For this, Sivanandhan created training centers across the state. A huge state-of-the-art training center was created in the cinema theater complex on Ghodbunder Road with the gift of a huge room from the Thane Municipal Corporation (TMC). It was appropriately furnished and called Manthan, meaning churning (of the minds). Many useful training programs were, and continue to be, held here successfully. Another world-class auditorium with training facilities, called Prerna, was created at the Mumbai Police Gymkhana.

The Maharashtra Intelligence Academy in Pune is another up-to-date training center with good infrastructure, to help hone intelligence-gathering skills.

▶ **Dedication to work**

Thane Police School: Among the entire infrastructure he created during his police career, one building is very close to Sivanandhan's heart. It is a building he is proud to have created. This building stands strong for policemen and will benefit generations to come. It is the Thane Police School. He was already instrumental in building two police schools at Gadchiroli and Chandrapur while he was Deputy Inspector General of Police, Nagpur range.

How does one guarantee that an employee remains devoted to his work? It is not by paying large sums of money or by enforcing a law. It comes from the employee's feeling that someone is taking care of him, that someone is concerned about the matters that he is concerned about.

By building the Thane school, Sivanandhan sent a message to the policemen that their children's education was also a priority. Sivanandhan felt strongly that the vicious cycle of police constables' children in turn becoming police constables ensured that future generations remained confined within the 10/10 room and mired in poverty. His dream was to see them becoming doctors, engineers and IAS/IPS officers. When this feeling comes naturally to every policeperson's mind, people feel devoted to their work.

The story of the reconstruction of this almost-defunct school is one of hope and vision, of transformation, of looking for the solution within the problem.

This was in 2005, when Sivanandhan was the Commissioner of Police (CP) of Thane. He was in his office doing routine work, when a lady came to visit him. She was a school teacher of the police school in Thane and wanted to resign.

She explained that she was disillusioned by the dismal working conditions in the school. She was the only teacher and the school had no facilities to speak of. Therefore, no new students were enrolling in the school.

The teacher in Sivanandhan took up this challenge. He immediately decided to visit the school, which was across the road outside the CP's office, along with the teacher.

The school which was built in 1920 had one teacher, 80 children, one room, no toilets, no fans, no lights. They deserved something better.

What he saw was not a problem but a solution. The land on which the school stood was huge and owned by the police department. Sivanandhan envisioned converting the out-of-use school to a world-class facility.

The land was owned by the police; that was a good starting point. He knew there was a golden opportunity here to create a future for the next generation of policemen. But to get gold from the mine, hard work and a proper process is required. He did not lose time, but began planning and setting things in motion.

He made a few phone calls and checked the legal provisions. He did his financial calculations and considered which people were likely to support the cause. Within a few days, the vision was crystal clear in his mind. It was possible.

He got the clearances and government approvals, the school affiliations as well as like-minded people to support the cause. The work began on March 1, 2005 and by June 15, the school began functioning. On December 19, 2005, a Shiamak Davar dance program yielded ₹ 3.5 crores from the public. By August 15, 2006, the 40,000 sq.ft. school stood ready in its full glory. It was inaugurated by then Home Minister Sri RR Patil, in the presence of the guardian minister Sri Ganesh Naik and all other public representatives. At last, the policemen owned their own school! The school was ready with all the facilities in just a few months.

When the school was started, it was bigger than before and had many more facilities. Therefore, it was decided that 50% of the seats in the school would be reserved for the children of policemen at subsidized fees. Now, about 3,000 children study in the school. The police children pay only 25% of the fees. No donations are taken from anybody. For the last four years, the school boasts of 100% results with first class and distinction in the Standard X examinations.

Due to the growing demand of admissions, now a few more floors have been added to the school. There is a rush for admissions and even non-police children seek admission there with an ever-increasing waiting list.

The school has flourished with time and is now among the most sought-after schools in Thane. The school's students have excelled in academics and sports; and parents see a bright future for their children. Please visit *www.thanepoliceschool.com* – a website created by Sivanandhan to know more.

Sivanandhan's moment of great happiness was when he got a call from a subordinate. "Sir, the policemen and their wives are upset that they are not getting admissions for their children in our school. The 50% seats that are allocated for the children of policemen are not enough to meet the demand. Their request is – stop giving seats to outside children. We want 100% seats for the children of policemen!"

Sivanandhan smiled. He recalled the day when a school teacher had walked in to his office, determined to resign. And he felt elated on receiving a call from a policeman demanding more seats to admit more children. His dream had become a reality.

▶ Loyalty and Honesty

Libraries: Books are a great source of information, knowledge and wisdom. Books can be found in most police stations, but most of these are technical and related to the job, such as police manuals, the Indian Penal Code, the Indian Constitution and various legal and other reference books.

However, to grow mentally and intellectually, the policeperson needs to read other good books on self-development, management, fiction and even biographies of inspiring men and women.

For this purpose, Sivanandhan created various libraries for policepersons wherever he served. About 10,000 inspiring books were purchased and policepersons were encouraged to read and start thinking of fresh ideas.

Sivanandhan himself is a voracious reader, and the same trait can be seen in both his daughters. A challenge his wife used to face during transfers was which books to take along and which to leave behind. Their houses were loaded with books and he gave away books very generously, encouraging others to read and grow.

He created the same atmosphere in the police department through the various libraries. In his opinion, a policeman would become wiser by reading various books, than just tackling problems that come to him when he wears the uniform.

Sivanandhan's plan to create a reading culture is very strategic in nature. Once a person starts reading about the lives and experiences of great people, their thoughts automatically become a part of yours. Thus, values such as loyalty and honesty gradually become a part of the reader's thinking and mindset.

You too can transform any scenario if you have the vision and a higher cause to fulfill. No problem is a problem till you see it yourself. Then you work on the solutions. And without realizing it, you start doing the impossible. You become the change and create the change.

So far in this book, we have seen the implementation of various projects. But no project, however strong the vision behind it, can be completed without financial support.

How a leader tackles this challenge is something we will see in the next chapter, which, according to Chanakya, is the next secret of leadership — *Kosha* (Finance or treasury).

★ TIPS TO BUILD GOOD INFRASTRUCTURE ★

1. Build world-class facilities: Do not compromise. Take up the challenge.

2. Focus on hard and soft infrastructure: Create an environment which is classy.

3. Take others' help: With inputs from others, you can make it better and faster.

4. Your vision should continue: If you have seen the benefit of creating something, make it for others as well.

5. Create landmark projects: In the problem itself lies the solution.

The Leader in Me

Notes

Chapter 5

Kosha

TREASURY/FINANCE

Swami	the king
Amatya	the minister
Janpada	the country
Durg	the fortified city
Kosha	**the treasury**
Dand	the army
Mitra	the ally

PART A

THE FIFTH SECRET

Kosha: Finance

KOSHA IS THE treasury that keeps the kingdom going. Chanakya has said that the first task of the king is to focus on the acquisition, growth and expansion of the treasury.

The treasury or finance maintains the kingdom and helps in its growth and expansion.

Chanakya has suggested in the *Arthashastra* that a king should have a sound understanding of economics; it is among the first subjects a king should learn. In the daily timetable of a king, the first activity should be checking the accounts of the kingdom.

The *koshadhyaksha*, or the finance head, must bring in daily reports and inform the king about the kingdom's financial situation. The king cannot lose focus on the finances.

Artha is wealth and *shastra* is scripture. Therefore, the *Arthashastra* itself means the scripture of wealth. Scholars have called it a book of economics that covers microeconomics and macroeconomics, accounting systems, auditing rules, collection of taxes and fines and utilization of public funds for the development of a kingdom.

It is a misconception that India and Indians do not understand much about money, economics and the practical ways of life. It is often believed that since Indians are spiritual, they think more about life after death, heaven, *moksha*, etc., than about wealth and material possessions.

However, India and Indians understand money and wealth like no other culture does. We know its practical value and also its limitations.

Why do you think we were the most prosperous nation and a target for invaders from all over the world? For thousands of years, we were the wealthiest nation and had even evolved a theory of economics which the Western world has not even understood.

The *Arthashastra* is proof of this. It is a book on wealth and its management. It is about knowledge of wealth and it is a wealth of knowledge. A study of the *Arthashastra* helps us to understand our past in all its glory. Principles of wealth described in the *Arthashastra* can be directly applied to modern-day situations.

Whether in the past or in the present, finance is the backbone of any undertaking. Every individual, family, society, organization and nation is dependent on money and finances. A strong and well-managed treasury is the heart of any organization.

The treasury is the basis on which the government creates national and state budgets. Budget-making is a highly specialized activity, which incorporates opinions from experts and guidelines on economic policy given by the Reserve Bank of India.

Good economic policies create employment and a conducive environment for the growth of trade, business and entrepreneurship.

Thus, good control and management of the treasury leads to the prosperity of the king, the citizens and the kingdom.

Once, a mother, who was very upset about her son not being able to make a good life, came to an ashram. She said to the head monk, "Guruji, my son was not good at studies; he could not get a good job to earn a livelihood. So, no one is ready to marry him. Since he is a failure in worldly matters, I think he is fit to be a monk. I want him to join your ashram."

The head monk replied, "Lady, being a monk does not mean escaping from the realities of the world. It is meant for those who are successful in worldly matters and want to go beyond. A person who cannot prove himself in the world outside, cannot be a winner in the world inside."

Thus, to be successful in this world, one has to work hard to prove oneself and earn money. Before one can renounce wealth and power, one has to earn it.

A very thin person was once watching a wrestling match. At the end of the match, the winner challenged the audience, "Is there anyone who wants to wrestle with me?"

This thin man excitedly accepted the challenge. However, when he reached the wrestling ring, he realized his blunder. His opponent was huge and well-built. The very first blow would have been enough to throw the thin man out of the ring.

The audience was laughing and waiting for this man to be smashed to pieces. To save his skin, the thin man came up with an idea. Just as the match was about to begin, he said to his opponent, "Please go away. I forgive you; I will not fight with you," and he ran away.

Many of us are like this thin man. The challenge excites us, but the reality is difficult to face. One very important reality of life is to earn money. Therefore, those who are unable to earn money find such justifications as, "I do not require money," "Money is evil," or "All rich people are thieves." This is a case of sour grapes.

A leader understands the importance of money. A responsible person will never underestimate the value of money.

Another important dimension of money is to be "money-conscious" and not "money-minded". A money-conscious person understands the importance of money and gives the right place and value to it.

A money-minded person, however, views the world from a financial perspective. The outlook of such people is ROI (return on investment) in every project. Their attitude is, "What is in it for me?"

Money-minded people look for direct or indirect financial benefits even in the social-work projects they undertake. Everything starts and ends with money for them. They draw their powers from their bank balances and value an individual based on his financial standing. The world for them becomes a deal-making platform.

For money-conscious people, money is a resource. It is a means to an end, not the end itself. They respect money. They work on finances, but understand that the vision of any project is more important than the finance itself.

These people are industrious; they are risk takers; they work for the benefit of society. They are the leaders and the role models who create positive change.

The *Arthashastra* details a financial model called the **Four Stages of Wealth**. This model can be applied to an individual as well as an organization.

The four stages of wealth are:

1. Wealth Identification

2. Wealth Creation

3. Wealth Management

4. Wealth Distribution

These are four stages in the journey to understand wealth in all its dimensions. This is the essence of all finance courses.

Let us discuss each stage of wealth.

1. Wealth Identification

Identification of wealth is the starting point.

To understand this better, suppose you want to dig a well. You will need to follow a scientific and logical process to understand the location of water levels underground, the land conditions, the depth at which water can be found and so on. When you dig a well armed with this knowledge, you are sure to find water.

Similarly, if you want to be wealthy, you need to research and find out areas of creating wealth. You can take the help of experts for this. Following the right direction and path is important to get to your destination faster.

Businessmen are always on the lookout for potential expansion opportunities. Financial investors work on identifying new sectors and industries that could provide good returns on investment. Salesmen try to identify new markets for their products and services. All these are examples of wealth identification.

Students often ask their teachers for guidance on courses to apply for, in order to build a career. In this case too, the student is trying to identify a long-term career opportunity.

Thus, identification is the first step. But simply identifying where the wealth is does not guarantee the wealth is yours.

After identifying the location of the water bed, the next step is to start digging the well.

2. Wealth Creation

Creating wealth is hard work. It is a laborious task that requires patience and a long-term perspective.

When you start digging the well, you work into an unknown future. Many times, there is self- doubt about whether you are working in the right direction and whether you will succeed.

You may also be subjected to the scrutiny and ridicule of others. This is where self-motivation is important.

The famous saying, "Winners never quit, and quitters never win" is useful here. Once you have carefully thought through your options and identified the wealth you are seeking, you need to work hard in that direction. It will be a long and tedious journey. But in spite of the hurdles, your hard work will pay off and you will succeed.

When we study about the lives of successful people, we appreciate the success, but sometimes forget the hard work they have put in to reach where they are.

A media person once asked a successful person, "Sir, you became a success overnight. How did you do it?" Came the reply, "Yes, I became a success overnight. But the night was very long."

Everyone wants to be wealthy. But creating wealth is the difficult part. If you want to be wealthy, remember, "There is no shortcut to success."

Once you strike gold, once you have created wealth, the whole world changes. You have tasted success; you have arrived.

3. Wealth Management

The end of one problem is the beginning of another. Once you have overcome the challenge of creating wealth, the new challenge is what to do with the money.

Initially, you were chasing money; now, money chases you. The tide has turned.

Success is relative — it brings many new relatives. People want to associate with you. You are surrounded by new friends. The world recognizes your success and wants to identify with you. Bankers and financial experts want to manage your wealth and offer you various investment options.

You should enjoy the money and success you have earned after years of hard work. But after the party is over, it is time for some serious thinking.

The challenge is to manage your wealth such that you can sustain it. You need not worry about basic survival issues now; you need to focus on maintaining your wealth.

This is where you need wealth management. With proper planning and good advice, you can start taking the right steps for a brighter future.

Managing the wealth you have created is as important as creating the wealth. If, like other wealthy people, you spend all your wealth as quickly as you earn it, you will very soon be back to square one. Instead, you need to save, invest and manage your wealth.

4. Wealth Distribution

Chanakya says, distribute the wealth you have created. Give it back to the underprivileged. Support a needy person, a start-up entrepreneur, a social cause, an artist, the education of a child, the health of an impoverished person.

This is easier said than done. Once you have enjoyed the power and glory that money gives you, it is not easy to let go. Without your realizing it, need becomes greed.

However, after leading a good and successful life, take up a new challenge to help people achieve what you have achieved.

True social service is not about helping others; it is helping yourself to evolve spiritually by letting go of your possessions. Share the secret of your success with others. Their success should become your success.

However, remember the story of the thin person who said to the wrestler, "I forgive you!" You cannot distribute wealth before you have identified, created and managed it.

Once you have gone through the three prior stages, when you distribute your wealth, it will be out of inner fulfillment and not regret.

In India, we give wealth a divine status by calling it Goddess Lakshmi and worshipping it. We are the only country in the world, which has given money a spiritual form. We consider it a blessing.

With the money you have created, fulfill your corporate social responsibility (CSR) and personal social responsibility (PSR). Only then would you have fulfilled your spiritual responsibility (SR).

As far as finance is concerned, Chanakya has brilliant advice to give us. In Book 2, Chapter 8, Verses 1-2 of the *Arthashastra*, he says,

"All undertakings are dependent first on the treasury. Therefore, he (the leader) should look to the treasury first."

Any project or assignment is dependent on finance. Great ideas cannot become reality if the required finance is not available.

"All undertakings" is very important. Be it a national project like building roads and bridges, or a small event at home like a birthday party or a television to be purchased, they are dependent on the treasury, that is, finance.

Chanakya then advises the leader, "Therefore, he should look into the treasury first."

The leader has to look at what is available in the treasury. For example, before you go shopping, you need to consider your bank balance and accordingly decide how much money can be spent.

The credit card system has changed this thinking drastically. We tend to look at the product first, and not the treasury, assuming that we can pay for the product later. According to Chanakya, we need to look at the treasury before finalizing the product and its purchase.

In an organization, the subordinates often have various plans and wishes, such as organizing a party or moving to a new office. While the subordinates' enthusiasm is important, the leader has to do his calculations and look at the finances.

However, if you find that you do not have the finances for a project suggested by your subordinate and beneficial to the organization, do not refuse outright. A response such as "It is not possible because we do not have the money for it," or "We have never undertaken such a big project," would demotivate employees and discourage them from sharing their ideas with you. As a leader, you should inspire innovation and creativity in your organization, not discourage it.

Therefore, if the project seems worthwhile, think about how to raise money for it. This is where leadership is important: making the impossible possible.

As Robert Kiosaki, the well-known expert and author on wealth, money and investment advises, "Think about possibilities of how to create that money which is required but you do not have."

The first step in raising or creating the money is to do your calculations and create a budget. This is a very important step, as you will see from the following anecdote.

Once, a wealthy person observed a creative, young boy working on a new engineering model. The person went up to the boy and said, "I am ready to help you financially. Let me know how much money is required." For the young boy, this was a dream come true.

However, he was not trained to think financially and could not estimate how much money he would need. He was surprised that someone had offered to finance his project so readily, but shocked that he himself had no idea how much it would cost.

He asked the wealthy man for a day's time. After doing his calculations, he submitted a project report the next day. Within a few minutes, he received a check for the full amount.

Creativity and imagination without budgeting is building castles in the air. Getting the finances right is a step towards making your dream castle a reality.

Here is an anecdote about the importance of budgeting and finance, especially for budding entrepreneurs.

A businessman was going through tough times. New orders were not coming in; existing orders were not getting executed. He was not able to pay his vendors, which affected the raw material supply. His clients were not paying on time because of quality issues in the products delivered. Employees were quitting the company due to non-payment of salaries.

The tough financial situation affected his domestic life too and he found it difficult to make both ends meet.

Despite all his efforts, the crisis did not seem to end. In sheer frustration, he thought of the final solution to all his problems: ending his life.

So, one morning, he left for office as usual, bidding goodbye to his family. But instead of going to the office, he went to the seashore. It was tough to end his life, but it also seemed like the only solution.

He wrote a suicide note, stating that nobody but himself was to blame for the act. And now, he was ready to walk into the water which would take him away from his worldly responsibilities forever.

As he took the first step, he saw an old man standing in front of him, smiling mischievously.

He wondered whether the person was one of his many creditors and why he was smiling. The old man came closer, and with a twinkle in his eye, asked, "Suicide?"

The businessman thought, "I am in no mood to listen to your philosophy of life. I don't want you to tell me life is precious and all that. I have tried everything and this is the only way out."

As he prepared to say this to the old man, the old man piped in, "Let's come straight to the point. You are in a financial mess and cannot see a way out. Right?"

The man was surprised. "Who is this man? He hit the nail on the head," was his immediate thought.

But again, before he could say anything, the old man said, "I have a solution to offer."

"Oh my God, he's probably an insurance agent or financial advisor. Get lost, man! I have no time or mental energy to listen to your expert advice," thought the man angrily. "Why can't people let you commit suicide in peace? God, this is not fair at all!"

"How much money do you require?"

"What?" The man was finally able to get a word out. "But sir, I do not know you."

"That doesn't matter," said the old man. "I am a businessman too and like to come straight to the point. Can we talk?"

They sat on the seashore and after a long time, the businessman was able to think, rather than worry. He had met a man who could contribute.

The businessman was all ears as the old man began, "Money is never the cause of evil or good. It is neutral. If it goes into the hands of bad people, it becomes dirty money and can cause destruction. In the hands of good people, it is used for good causes and becomes divine.

"Understanding money makes us wise. If there is a financial problem, it is important to face it. It is important to be practical and look for a solution," he continued.

"A person running a house, organization or nation needs to obtain and manage finances carefully. If he does not get the foundations right, it can create a disaster, and even lead to the thought of suicide," he continued with his mischievous smile.

He paused to let the businessman think this over and asked again, "How much money do you need?"

"Sir, I do not understand," the businessman said in a mellow voice.

"Have you calculated how much money you need to pay your vendors, suppliers, employees and other bills at home?"

"Not really, sir. But I have given up hope."

"That is not the point. Did you do your calculations?" the old man asked sternly. "In such a mental state, it may not be possible for you to do this alone. So, let us do it together. Here is a pen and paper; start writing."

Surrendering to his new-found mentor's wishes, the businessman listed his debts and reached a figure of ₹ 2 crore.

The old man said, "Good, we have completed the first step. When life gives us complex problems, write them down and think on paper. Then, look for practical solutions.

"Now, the next step is to think about sources of money," the old man continued.

The businessman said, "Sir, I have tried everything – more credit time from vendors, bank loans for working capital, everything. But, it is all over now."

"What if I give you the money?"

The businessman could not believe his ears. Why would this old man help an unknown person, without any guarantee of getting his money back?

But the old man continued, "I will give you the money you require, without any expectation in return, no interest or guarantees, no bonds to be signed." The businessman was dumbfounded.

The old man introduced himself as Pravin Chheda, the chairman of Gurudev Steel Industries. "In my long career of over 50 years, I have built an empire. I have also seen many businessmen losing their confidence and committing suicide because of lack of financial support during tough times," he explained.

He continued, "Fortunately, in the days when I was struggling, other rich businessmen helped me. Today, I do the same thing to thank those who helped me.

"But there is one difference. I also help unknown people. Many of my friends tell me not to trust unknown people with money. But I have always taken risks — sometimes calculated, at other times, based on gut feel."

The old man gave an insight into how a wealthy man should think, "At times, your risk does not pay off. You lose money. But I look at the big picture. Even if one out of the ten people I helped succeeds, my work is done."

He added that he had an annual budget to help businessmen who were in financial trouble. "I call it the confidence building budget (CBD)," he said.

Though the businessman was skeptical about the offer, Mr Chheda offered to give him a check of ₹ 2.5 crore right there. "The extra money is to meet unexpected expenses. Take it. And do not worry about returning it. Focus on your business revival and progress."

"But Sir, this is too big an amount for me not to return," said the businessman hesitantly.

"And too small an amount for me to save a life and rebuild a business," Mr. Chheda replied. He wished the businessman good luck and said, "We will meet here after six months to review the situation."

After months of despair and frustration, the businessman's luck had finally turned. With the money in his hands, he felt confident of reviving his sagging fortunes.

Instead of going to office, he decided to go home and spend the rest of the day with his family. His family too could sense that he was calm and relaxed, not the agitated and frustrated person he had been for such a long time.

The next morning, he decided to deposit the check. As he was going to the bank, he thought, "When things get better, I would like to repay this money. I will consider this as a debt and give it back many times over."

Then, he thought that it would be a grand gesture if he did not use this money at all, but returned the check after six months, along with a second check from his earnings. That would justify the faith the old man had reposed in him.

However, he desperately needed money to pay his debts. He said to himself, "I have stretched myself to this extent. Let me test my limits some more. If things get worse, I can deposit this check any time."

He thought of an action plan to see if he could revive his business without using the check.

First, instead of running away from the situation, he called all his employees and gave them a reality update. "We are going through a rough patch, and I know your salaries have been delayed. But, I have a request — can you support me for just one more month?

"We will give it our best shot. Please continue to work a little harder and I promise you things will get better. All of us have worked together for many years and our business has goodwill built over many years. Let's try to rebuild the business.

I promise you I will pay your pending salaries, along with interest and bonus.

"You also have the option to take your pending salary and quit now." He had to just deposit the check. "I leave the decision to you," he concluded.

As he looked straight into their eyes, the employees sensed the seriousness of his intent and his honesty. They agreed to stay on for another month.

The commitment from your team boosts your morale. At times, the leader instills confidence in the team. And many times, the team makes leaders feel more confident of achieving their goals.

Next, he called his oldest vendor, "Sir, I know I owe you a lot of money. But if you can immediately supply just one more lot of raw material, I can start processing my pending orders. I promise, as soon as I receive the first check from my customers, I will start releasing money to you."

The vendor was surprised, because until then, the businessman had been avoiding his calls regarding the outstanding payment. Now, the businessman had himself asked for support and assured payment. Considering their long business relationship, the vendor decided to release the raw material.

The businessman's third action was to call the customer who had rejected several orders and not released payments because of quality issues. The businessman apologized for the quality issues and for defaulting on orders.

He continued confidently. "Sir, you were the first company to give me an order many years ago, and I have grown because of you. I request you to support me one more time." The businessman confided about cash-flow issues on his end and requested the customer to release some money as an on-account payment. "It will help me start the manufacturing process once again and supply the pending orders per your quality standards."

The customer sensed the businessman's sincerity and decided to help him. He called the accountant and asked him to release a check for ₹ 20 lakh.

Within a few minutes, the businessman had the key ingredients in place. He immediately started work and his team — employees, salespersons, quality control persons — worked day and night with him to rebuild the company.

Within one month, the situation was very different. When the first lot of finished goods reached the customer, he was more than satisfied and was happy to release some more money. The businessman took the help of experts to analyze the old, rejected goods and fix the quality issues. The goods were then sent back to the customer in accordance with the expected quality standards.

The customer was delighted. New orders started coming in. Word spread in the market. New customers started approaching the businessman directly. The sales team started working closely with the production department. And they turned the tide.

Every morning, the businessman used to look at the check he had got from the old man. He was happy it was not deposited.

With time, the business grew from strength to strength. The businessman was able to pay his employees in full, with interest and bonuses as promised. He was now looking at setting up another manufacturing unit and hiring more people.

Six months after his first meeting with Mr Chheda, the businessman returned to the same seashore for their promised meeting. He had brought the original check with him and an additional check to thank Mr Chheda for his support.

When Mr Chheda arrived, the businessman touched his feet. "Sir, thank you so much for all the help. I am glad you saved my life and my business." He handed over the original check of ₹ 2.5 crore and the additional check of ₹ 25 lakh to thank him.

But Mr Chheda said, "Keep the second check. Use this money to help someone who has financial problems, the way you faced problems six months ago. And when you give it away, do not expect any returns."

The businessman agreed to do so. However, he had been struggling with a question for a while now and decided to ask the old man.

"Sir, I did not have money when I met you six months ago. And I never used your money. As far as money is concerned, my situation was the same. So, what changed for me to revive my business?"

Mr Chheda had seen many such turnarounds in his life. So, it was easy for him to point out, "Money is a tool. The person using the money is more important than the money itself. But, a good estimation of finances gives you the right starting point.

"In your case, what you lacked was confidence. And money was required to build that confidence. I gave you the money and you bounced back. I am glad you rebuilt your business with that confidence, rather than the money I gave you."

Mr Chheda continued, "This is called call-money in business. Call-money is commonly used in community businesses or rural areas. You see, when a young businessman starts a new venture, he requires support."

He was now letting the businessman into a secret that many professional MBAs did not know. "The biggest support is when a group of people back the idea. This is the greatest confidence builder. In most cases, a person may not give you the money to start with, but when someone says, 'I am with you,' that itself is a wonderful starting point."

He explained further, "Say a project requires ₹ 1 crore. Five people would verbally commit ₹ 20 lakh each to the entrepreneur. This is call-money. That commitment itself is enough to set the entrepreneur on track.

"The entrepreneur will still raise the money through a bank loan or other sources. But, if other sources fail him, he knows he can always fall back on any of these five businessmen.

"In most cases, the entrepreneur is able to get some support, in cash or kind, such as office space, a supply of raw materials, or even a first order. Thus, the young entrepreneur starts off. In most cases, the call-money is not used at all."

Then, he came to the crux of the matter, "Call-money is never real money. It is a state of mind." Smiling, he continued, "But then, what is really required in life is the confidence of money, not necessarily the money itself."

This story is very important for young entrepreneurs. If you have a good idea, go to senior businessmen and explain the concept. Their blessings are enough. In India, this has been a practice for many generations.

Call-money is also called "financial closure" in modern businesses. Once a project plan and cost estimations are ready, it is announced to various people, some of whom would commit finances to the project. Once the finances are closed, it is easy to start up with full speed.

PART B

ACCORDING TO CHANAKYA

Qualities of a Good Treasury

IN BOOK 6, Chapter 1, Verse 10 of the *Arthashastra*, Chanakya says, the *kosha* should have the following qualities:

▶ Acquired lawfully by ancestors and oneself

▶ Able to withstand calamity

▶ Can be sustained even when there is no income for long time

The *Arthashastra* was written nearly 2,400 years ago. There have been many changes since then in financial models, institutions and transaction methods. Financial institutions like banks have come up. From coinage, we have moved to currency notes, check books and plastic cards. The internet helps us in e-banking and mobile banking.

Yet, the principles of money and wealth do not change with time. They are eternal, constant, time-tested laws.

There is a reason why many ancient scriptures like the *Arthashastra*, *Ramayana*, *Mahabharata* and *Thirukkural* are still read and referred to by a globalized and tech-savvy generation. The laws and principles described in these scriptures are universally applicable even today.

With that knowledge, let us take a closer look at Chanakya's description of the *kosha*.

▶ Acquired lawfully by ancestors and oneself

This is the first principle of money. It must be acquired lawfully. Wealth that is acquired by unlawful and unethical means does not last long. Even if it stays with you, you lose your peace of mind. To enjoy wealth, it has to be acquired by lawful and ethical means. It is not wrong to make big money, as long as it is through the right means. This also means paying due taxes and not cheating others.

Growing rich and making a quick buck is the in-thing today. Many people do not pay attention to the methods used to acquire wealth. But remember, there are no shortcuts to success. Ramdeo Agarwal, a financial wizard, says in the film *Chanakya Speaks*, "Wealth that takes longer to create stays for a longer period."

Thus, wealth that comes quickly goes away quickly. But the wealth that is earned through hard work is real wealth. Wealth could also be acquired by your ancestors and you may be fortunate enough to inherit it. Some people are destined to be born in wealthy families owing to the merits of their past lives.

However, inheriting wealth does not mean squandering it. Chanakya's advice is to expand the inherited wealth, not reduce it. What you have is the gift of your ancestors; if you grow it further, your ancestors will be happy. Children have the responsibility to grow the wealth that was given by their parents.

If you inherited a company worth ₹ 100 crore, try to increase its worth to ₹ 500 crore, rather than reducing it to ₹ 50 crore. Kumar Mangalam Birla was only 26 years old when he inherited the company from his father, who met with an untimely death. The valuation of the Aditya Birla group today is many times what it was during his father's time. Is there any doubt that such a son is a role model to children born in business families?

Make a lot of money, but through the right means. Be slow but sure. You may fail in your first few attempts, but do not get disheartened. Keep trying; do not be afraid of making mistakes. Chanakya says, "After a hundred trials, you will succeed."

▸ **Able to withstand calamity**

Financial ups and downs are a part of life, irrespective of whether a person is rich or poor. For the poor, financial problems are related to the basic necessities of survival; for the rich, problems are related to maintaining and growing their wealth.

Therefore, it is important to plan your finances such that you can withstand calamities. A futuristic viewpoint, rather than immediate gratification, is required for that. You need to "sustain" your wealth for the future.

The age-old Indian concept of "savings" is applicable here. India was able to hold its own during the global recession not just due to government's measures or economists' advice, but because of individuals' propensity to save.

The Indian culture believes in saving. As an agricultural country dependent on the monsoon, we have always saved our farm produce to sustain us for the rest of the year. With economic development, savings took the form of money or gold.

There is a difference between savings and investments. Savings is the first step while investment is the next level. Save for the rainy day, and invest for growth.

The difference between savings and investment is very subtle, yet profound. A poor man cannot invest for growth. He needs to save for the next meal. Only money that is left over after taking care of basic needs can be invested.

Investment is a science in itself. It requires a different bent of mind to be a successful investor. Successful investors are thinkers who take calculated risks. Investment should never be an impulsive decision. It should be carefully thought through. Your hard-earned money should be invested in the right place, at the right time and also on the right person.

Insurance is one more concept to understand here. You may not have money enough to invest, but you should insure yourself. A poor man cannot afford to invest, but he should insure himself and his family. Life insurance and medical insurance are safety nets that help to take care of you and your family in times of calamity.

Governments across the globe are working on insurance for their people. Companies insure their employees. A person should insure his family, wealth and property. The amount spent on insurance is minimal compared to the benefits that will follow in case there is a calamity.

Save – Insure – Invest. These are the three steps that will help you to withstand any crisis.

▶ **Can be sustained even when there is no income for long time**

In life, you may face long periods of misfortune.

For example, a poor, uneducated woman suddenly loses her husband and has no social support to speak of. She has to work hard, take care of the household and educate her children.

She knows her capacity to earn is limited because she is not very educated. So, her only hope of improving her family's lot is to educate her children and improve their career prospects.

This is a long-term approach to finance. If she takes a short-term approach and asks her children to take up employment right away, their future would be compromised.

Financial wisdom is working hard even if there is no income in the short term. In the long run, the hard work will pay off and good times will return.

Some businesses are seasonal in nature, yet salaries to employees must be paid every month. For example, during the Diwali season, sales of fireworks, dresses and cars increase manifold. Some companies prepare for their Diwali season sales almost six months in advance.

In these six months, while they are manufacturing the goods, they have to bear the costs of manufacturing, including salaries to employees, with little or no income. The owner of such a company cannot withhold payments until he is able to sell the goods and earn money. Finally, during the sale season, cash inflow far exceeds cash outflow.

Such a long-term approach requires patience and financial wisdom.

It is often said that "A businessman should plan 10 years ahead, a politician one generation ahead, and a teacher a century ahead."

PART C

LEADERSHIP IN ACTION

Financial Management
is the Key to Success

Wealth is the product of man's capacity to think.

AYN RAND IN *ATLAS SHRUGGED*

Money can be raised through various means. In this case study, you will see how Sivanandhan's financial management of the various projects he undertook is a shining example of the qualities of a good treasury described by Chanakya.

▶ **Acquired lawfully by ancestors and oneself**

Sivanandhan ensured that money spent on projects was always collected through legal sources. In the case of the police department, there were two major legal sources — government grants and budgets, and social support, that is, fundraisers or corporate social responsibility (CSR) activities of various companies. Sivanandhan made ample use of both sources.

The challenge, however, was to make sure that there was a win-win situation for both the giver and the taker.

CSR initiatives included setting up of schools, hospitals, restaurants, training centers, gymnasiums and stadiums.

Additionally, a cyber-crime cell was instituted and anti-terrorism seminars were organized.

Some projects were landmarks by themselves. The police training center at Thane named Manthan, was constructed in a hall given to the Thane police by the Thane Municipal Corporation (TMC), in exchange for the assistance rendered by the police in handling a law and order situation that arose from the TMC's waste management projects. Manthan has a seating capacity of more than 200 with state-of-the-art training facilities. The center cost nearly ₹ 3 crore. Another example was the training center, Prerna, constructed at South Mumbai with the support of various well-wishers.

He not only organized funds for what he felt was needed, but took regular feedback from his people, asking them for suggestions for improvement. A traffic policeman once suggested installing an oxygen booth for policemen, who manage traffic on congested roads amid high levels of air pollution.

In the next 10 days, Sivanandhan organized funds, convincing Essel World to sponsor the oxygen booth that cost ₹ 65,000.

The state-of-the-art hospital at Thane was constructed at a cost of ₹ 1.5 crore. The dental machines at the hospital were sponsored by a corporate house. Sivanandhan negotiated with the Wockhardt group of hospitals to run it for the police. The hospital's facilities are provided free of cost for the 6,000 police families of the Thane Police.

Considering his noble intentions, various individuals and organizations also came forward to help Sivanandhan financially. Yoga classes and Art of Living workshops were conducted for the police free of cost by the respective organizations.

▶ **Able to withstand calamity**

When he was the CP of Thane City (2005–2008), he opened a cyber-crime cell and cyber-crime laboratory in his office in Thane. ₹ 17 lakh were spent by NASSCOM to create this cell, which was later also created for the Mumbai police.

It was important to understand future crime trends and make plans to withstand these calamities. Sivanandhan's plan to create a cyber-crime cell is an answer to withstand future calamities that may arise through cyber crimes.

▶ **Can be sustained even when there is no income for a long time**

During his interaction with his subordinates, Sivanandhan evolved some incentive schemes for his force. However, he realized that if a policeman is given an additional ₹ 2,000, he may spend it on buying a mobile phone or bike, or on liquor and other unproductive activities. Therefore, providing good education to policemen's children was a better option.

He also realized that policemen who wanted to admit their children to reputed schools often had to pay ₹ 50,000 to ₹ 1 lakh as donation, which many of them could not afford.

He came to the conclusion that if the policemen were to be liberated from this vicious cycle of poverty, education was the only means. Therefore, instead of extra salary increments, it was better to create a world-class educational institution. This was also the inspiration behind the Thane Police School.

Sivanandhan had a long-term perspective. He realized that the problem of poverty would not be solved by merely giving money to the policemen. The idea was to eliminate poverty itself. Building an educational institution was a long-term solution to ensure long-term income.

In designing the Thane Police School, Sivanandhan decided to provide all the amenities and facilities from the beginning itself, rather than building the school piecemeal, grade by grade. Time was of the essence; he wanted the school to be fully operational before he was posted elsewhere.

To fulfill this grand vision, Sivanandhan arranged a fundraiser program by Shiamak Davar in December 2005. Though he had spent about 10 months in Thane, he received overwhelming support from the public. The fundraiser was a runaway success, earning about ₹ 3.5 crore. The profit of ₹ 3.5 crore was used to build the school.

Visit *www.thanepoliceschool.com* to see the making of the school. The school is run by the Goenka Educational Trust. It is one of the finest schools in the area with state-of-the-art infrastructure and does not accept any donations for admission of students.

While Sivanandhan raised funds and helped build several facilities during his tenure at Thane, he also wanted to ensure that these facilities would be maintained well by his successors. That would require finance in the long term. Therefore, a Police Welfare Fund was created for this purpose. The operations of Urjita Restaurant — which had been built in the Thane headquarters to provide policemen with better-quality food served in a hygienic place with good ambience — were rented out to a private operator at around ₹ 1 lakh per month. This rent became part of the Police Welfare Fund. Nearly ₹ 12 lakh for the Fund was received each year from rent alone.

The creation of the Welfare Fund allowed Sivanandhan's successors to maintain the Thane Police School, the stadium he built and various other structures. Therefore, long-term planning of finances helped to build and maintain infrastructure.

As we have seen, money is only a tool, a means to an end. Sivanandhan collected it through various sources and used it to create the best possible facilities for the police force.

Also, in terms of finances, it is important to inspire your team and give them credit.

Let us end this chapter with an incident about sharing your money and success with your team. We will go into more detail on this in the next chapter.

Sivanandhan was once invited by the Lions Club, which had nominated him for a police bravery award. Instead of receiving the award himself, Sivanandhan gave it to a hawaldar, Sanjay Manchekar who Sivanandhan felt had shown exemplary bravery in a case, who he felt truly deserved it.

Hawaldar Manchekar was posted to provide protection to the owners of a hotel in Mulund. A group of four gangsters came to shoot at the owners of the hotel. Manchekar jumped into action. The gangsters fired at Manchekar and ran away in an auto. Manchekar himself chased the gangsters in another auto and in four rounds of firing, ultimately succeeded in nabbing them, risking his own life in the process.

Sivanandhan felt that due recognition for such a hawaldar's action was more important. Manchekar was honored in a grand public function organized by the Lions Club on April 25, 1999, during the police bravery awards and he was presented a check of ₹ 5,000 along with a citation. It was a proud occasion for him and his family. Sanjay Manchekar, growing nostalgic over the event said, "It was a highly memorable moment for me. It boosted my morale and my pride in being a part of the police force."

Sivanandhan also spoke to the Commissioner of Police (CP) and got him a reward of ₹ 25,000 which was a very big amount in those days. Manchekar also got the DG's insignia.

The most important aspect is that Hawaldar Sanjay Manchekar was not a part of Sivanandhan's team.

Yet, Sivanandhan felt the strong need to give this recognition and appreciation. In a police force of lakhs of hawaldars, getting this recognition was a momentous achievement for Manchekar.

This is one of the examples of Sivanandhan's way of motivating his people.

★ TIPS FOR FINANCIAL MANAGEMENT ★

1. Consider multiple sources: You should be able to raise finance from various sources.

2. Goodwill is important: Along with goodwill, your personal integrity is important.

3. Work for others: Invest in projects that will be financially beneficial to everyone.

4. Think long term: Financial planning should encompass both creation and maintenance.

5. Share your wealth: Share it with others in your team who would otherwise never get the credit for the team's achievements.

The Leader in Me

Chapter 6

Dand

ARMY/TEAM

Swami	the king
Amatya	the minister
Janpada	the country
Durg	the fortified city
Kosha	the treasury
Dand	**the army**
Mitra	the ally

THE SIXTH SECRET

Dand: The Team

THE SIXTH PILLAR of a kingdom is the army. It showcases the power of a country and protects the citizens from external threats. Besides fighting outsiders, the army is also utilized during emergencies such as floods or to solve internal crises, as in the case of civil wars. Apart from the armed forces on the borders, the police force is the internal army of a country.

An army is a trained group of people that is ready to fight any threat. Appropriate selection and training are very important to build a strong army, as is the commitment and dedication of the soldiers.

"Army", in this book, will be interpreted as "team".

One man alone cannot fight a battle. It is always a team that wins a war. For example, while Satyajit Ray won an Oscar for his lifelong commitment to the art of filmmaking, the fact remains that an entire team comprising cameramen, financiers, technicians, artists and spot boys supported his endeavors. Thus, his team is as important as Satyajit Ray himself.

Similarly, in a cricket team, one player may score a century, hit a six on the last ball, win the game and be crowned the Man of the Match. Yet, the team's victory is due to the performance of all its players — the fielders, bowlers and other batsmen have all done their bit to win the match.

While one person may get credit for extraordinary performance; yet, it is finally teamwork that makes any person a winner.

In an organization, the chairman of the company is at the helm, and guides and gives direction to others. Yet, the entire team of managers, workers, vendors, office boys and drivers, work together for the growth and success of the company, to help the company achieve its objectives.

As the captain of the team, the leader is always given credit for the team's achievements. Yet, the leader should never forget to share the credit with team members. That is real leadership — to share your success with others.

In a team, different people have different mindsets. In fact, the strength of a team lies in its differences, rather than its similarities. When team members are able to think about issues from different angles and perspectives, then there is real debate and progress.

For example, a team is working towards a product launch and the group leader asks the team members for their opinions. Each member will have a different perspective about the product launch — one may consider the budget; another may think the timing of the launch was important; a third would focus on market segments; while a fourth may draw attention to the importance of attractive packaging. All of these viewpoints only help to make the product launch a success.

If all the team members think differently, what is common in the team? What keeps the team together? It is the purpose that keeps the team together. A cricket team's purpose is to win the match; a business team's objective is to offer its goods and services for a profit; a police force's purpose is to maintain law and order.

Thus, if different members of any team focus on the core purpose, in spite of their differences, they will stick together to achieve the goal for which they came together.

Teamwork begins with the leader. The leader should understand the importance of teamwork and instill the value of good teamwork in his team.

The famous army saying says, "The safety, honor and welfare of your country come first, always and every time. The honor, welfare and comfort of the men you command come next. Your own ease, comfort and safety come last, always and every time."

This statement summarizes the purpose of the army most aptly. The army works together for the country first. The next priority is the team members, who should be ready to sacrifice themselves for each other's welfare. Only after that can each individual think of his safety or comfort.

In a team, each member has different strengths and weaknesses. A leader should be able to understand the strengths and weaknesses of each team member, and allocate work to them accordingly.

If someone in the team has not completed the work as required, the leader has to question himself, "Did I delegate the work to the right person? Could someone else have done this better? Who else in my team is capable of doing this properly?"

A good leader is someone who gets work done from people who may not even think they were capable of doing it. Thus, the leader should have the subtle vision to understand a person better than the person understands himself.

After allocating work, the leader must continuously supervise the team. A leader can delegate work, but not his responsibility. If the team fails in its tasks, the leader has to shoulder the responsibility.

The captain of a sinking ship always leaves last, only after each person on the ship has been rescued.

Therefore, in the *Arthashastra*, Chanakya emphasizes that a leader has to be fully alert and regularly keep track of the work his people are doing.

For this, the leader should ask his subordinates to file status reports regularly. Today, these reports are titled Management Information Systems (MIS) and can be filed annually, monthly, weekly or even daily.

In the police department, one of the daily routines of the leader is to study these reports. The leader must supervise every detail of the team, from the attendance of each team member to the work he is doing. If the leader loses track, then it becomes difficult to plan and make strategies for meeting team objectives.

How does one create a good team or army of dedicated people?

The first step is selecting the right person, who has the requisite qualities and qualifications for that particular job. A farmer has to select the best seeds before he sows them. Therefore, the first step is to ensure the person who will join your team is the right person for the job. Testing the right person in the selection process itself is the key to success.

The next step is to train the person. The person should be a trainable person, that is, he should be open to change.

The selected person may have the capability, yet he is new to the job. You cannot expect productivity from him on day one. You have to train and give him enough opportunities to learn on the job.

In Book 1, Chapter 5, Verse 6 of the *Arthashastra*, Chanakya describes how to conduct training:

"Training and discipline are acquired by accepting the authority of the teachers in the respective fields."

Here is an analysis of this verse.

▶ Training

Creating a good team requires training. It is for this purpose that organizations have induction programs and the police force imparts entry-level training to new recruits.

People often find their training days to be among the best in their lives, because of the new skills they learn, and because these are carefree days with few responsibilities.

▶ Discipline

The trainee must focus on the purpose of the training and not take it casually.

During the training, the trainee may not have any work-related responsibilities, but he should remember that he is preparing for many future responsibilities. Therefore, the trainee should be disciplined from the start.

There are two kinds of discipline — external and internal. External discipline is imposed by the teachers and other senior authorities. Trainees often have to follow a code of conduct and are penalized if they break the rules.

This external discipline should lead to internal discipline or self-discipline. The trainee should not require the presence of senior authorities or the threat of penalties to demonstrate disciplined behavior.

The training and discipline should be with the trainee forever.

Discipline helps build character. It is an aura you carry with you, wherever you go. In the police force too, discipline is very important. Being punctual, dressing well, obeying seniors and not keeping any decisions pending are important aspects of being disciplined.

A disciplined person is respected everywhere, because he embodies certain values and principles and lives his life by them.

▶ Accepting the authority of teachers

Discipline can be difficult or easy to achieve.

Chanakya explains that it is easily achieved by accepting the authority of the teachers. That is, trainees must completely accept the teacher or trainer, and trust his maturity and experience.

There should not be any element of doubt about the teacher's knowledge when you are getting trained. If there is a conflict such as "Is my teacher saying the right thing?" or "I don't think this trainer or officer knows the subject well," then there is a problem.

The trainee's attitude should be like a child learning from the mother. Whatever the mother says, the child accepts as the ultimate truth. There is no iota of doubt. This type of connection between the trainee and the trainer leads to rapid learning.

If the trainee begins questioning the trainer's ability at the first stage itself, there is no progress. Questions should be asked after the trainee has achieved a degree of maturity and experience. Only then will the trainer's answers also be understood well.

This quality of tuning to the teacher is called *Shraddha* in Sanskrit. This word does not have an English equivalent. It is not belief or surrender; neither is it blind faith. It is a beautiful inner connection between the teacher and the student.

It is an inner transformation in the student when he "tunes" himself to the mental wavelength of the teacher. It is like a radio getting tuned to the right radio station. Then there are no more disturbances, the music is clear and one can listen to it for long hours.

During the training, it is important for the trainee to get totally tuned to the teacher and accept him as the authority in the field.

Students often blame teachers for not being able to teach well. There may be some element of truth in that, but students should also question if they were the right students.

One day, a child came home very angry and upset and told his mother, "Our geography teacher is very boring; she does not teach properly. All my friends in school also hate her."

The mother advised, "My child, there will be many more teachers in your life. Some may be able to communicate well; others may not be able to do so. Every teacher has a different method of teaching. Just because you did not like the method or style of teaching does not mean she is a bad teacher. From today onwards, you have to be a good student of geography."

The child was given a completely new perspective on how he should think in the classroom. From the next day, he was so tuned to the teacher that he topped the class in the exams.

▶ Respective fields

Teachers, whether in school or college, teach different subjects, that is, they are experts in their "respective fields". There are teachers and then there are specialist teachers. For example, a teacher of Sanskrit will teach the basics of the language, while a teacher of Sanskrit grammar will go deeper into the subject.

In today's generation of super-specialization, it is especially important for students to listen to and accept each teacher.

Sivanandhan was a professor of economics in his pre-police days. He enjoyed teaching and this passion continued for life. It continues in this book form to reach out to many who do not know him.

Even in his Indian Police Service (IPS) training days, experts in various fields came to teach the new recruits. Later, when

Sivanandhan became a leader himself, he continued training the force with the help of world-class teachers.

In this chapter, you will read about the various training initiatives taken by Sivanandhan to build a strong team.

There were days when one used to study to get a job. Nowadays, people study to maintain their jobs. Continuous training is essential in today's times.

One has to read textbooks in school and college to pass exams, but the habit of reading good books and acquiring knowledge all through life should be developed. You should be an ever-ready student and learn from every person who comes into your life.

Teamwork can be easily achieved if the leader is focused on training and development. Today, various organizations like the police have their own training centers. These are educational institutions which share knowledge with the team to perform better.

As the definition of TEAM goes, Together Each one Achieves More.

One person alone may not be strong, but ten weak people coming together is strength. Synergy is seen in good teamwork. Synergy is the concept of one plus one adding up to greater than two. When two ideas come together, the result is better than if the ideas were executed in isolation.

In teamwork, there is happiness instead of frustration, collaboration rather than competition, and acceptance instead of denial. The leader puts all of the individual team members together and achieves the goal. Then, all of them celebrate their achievements together.

PART B

ACCORDING TO CHANAKYA

Qualities of a Good Team

THE BEST WAY to learn teamwork is to observe nature. You will see many examples of teamwork.

A flock of birds in the sky follows the laws of aerodynamics in teamwork. The birds fly in a V-shaped formation. They are tuned to each other and follow the leader. When that leader gets tired, it goes behind and another bird becomes the leader. They help each other during the long flight and reach their destination peacefully.

Ants always work in groups. Forming a perfect line, like a parade, they march from one place to another. If a heavy piece of bread cannot be carried by one ant alone, they help each other. An anthill is a community staying together. They work hard during the good times and collect food. During bad times, they share the food.

Crows also work in teams. When a crow sights food, it calls the other crows and they all eat together. Again, when a crow is in trouble, it calls the other crows. They protect the troubled one and take it to safety.

In human beings, teamwork is best observed in villages. The difference between a village and a city is often described as, "In a village, the first person knows the last person. And in a city, we don't even know our neighbors."

A village is a perfect unit of harmony and coexistence. If a new person comes into the village, everyone knows if he is an enemy or a friend. The village unites to fight an enemy and to welcome and take care of a friend.

Marriages in villages are also community events. Villagers share the responsibilities of the wedding too. Someone may sponsor the food; another person may be responsible for the decoration; and someone else may provide the vehicles required. The village works together as a team for the event.

Once, the marriage procession of the bridegroom, the *baaraat*, was returning from a village, without the marriage taking place. On being asked why, someone from the procession said that the bride's father could not afford to pay the dowry, which the bridegroom's party asked for at the last moment. Even though dowry is illegal, it is part of the wedding customs in some areas.

The bride's father was understandably upset. Suddenly, a wealthy man from the village announced, "Call the boy and his family back, and ask the *pandit* to conduct the marriage. I will pay the dowry right now!" He continued, "No *baaraat* has ever returned from our village and it will not happen this time too."

That is the association everyone in the community has with each other. They not only share happiness, but also sad times.

The joint family system in India is another example of teamwork. If a family had four sons, they all stayed together, along with their wives and children. The running of the house was a collective responsibility.

Irrespective of how much each one earned, all of them ate the same food. If one of the brothers could not earn due to an accident or unemployment, the remaining brothers made sure that he and his family were taken care of. Their children's upbringing, education and marriages were all held together.

A joint family system also offers security. In such a system, there is no requirement of a babysitter. The grandparents, aunts and elder cousins take care of the small children. Children find friends within their homes. They study together, play together, share their clothes and even celebrate festivals together. This is truly teamwork.

However, teamwork also means acceptance. You need to ignore the drawbacks of your team members, look at the positive aspects and move ahead in life. The formula is, "Together we succeed."

An ideal team has certain qualities, which Chanakya describes in the *Arthashastra* (Book 6, Chapter 1, Verse 11) as follows:

▶ Obedient

▶ Not disappointed during marches

▶ Able to face challenges

▶ Experienced in fighting battles

▶ Skilled in war and weapons

▶ Has no separate self-interest

If you want to develop a good team, develop these qualities in your team. If you already have these qualities, you are a good team and a role model.

Creating a good team starts with the leader. If the leader of a good team is bad, the team will get demotivated. On the other hand, a good leader can transform an ordinary team into an efficient team.

Now, let us look at the qualities of a good team in detail.

▶ Obedient

There could be hundreds of opinions, but there must be only one decision.

An ideal team is obedient and accepts the leader's decision. That means the team believes that the leader's decision is for the benefit of all. The team trusts the leader's wisdom to take the right decision for everyone.

If the leader is a man of integrity and values, he will look at the big picture and consider everyone's benefit.

Many leaders try to take decisions that will make them popular, but leadership is also about taking the tough call.

During police training, a person who is not obedient is punished. This punishment is to develop the quality of obedience. Before one becomes a good leader, he has to become a good follower. The leader in you will awaken only when you are an obedient follower.

This is the quality of *Shraddha* or perfect obedience again. Initially, you may not understand why a particular decision is taken. You may find it illogical and may not be convinced enough to do as the leader says. But in the long term, you will find that the decision was for the best.

A devotee, who worked under the great spiritual leader Swami Chinmayananda once recalled, "I worked as a manager of the ashram with him for many decades. In our meetings, he used to take decisions which we could never understand. At times, I used to rebel internally. Yet, I knew he was my guru and followed him without any questions. In the long run, I understood the reasons." He continued, "I could never prove him wrong!"

Leaders think differently. They have often seen and understood the matter much better than us. They have a wider outlook and have seen the big picture.

This is not to say that followers should not have any opinion of their own. Yet, followers have their limitations, and any decision taken from this limited outlook may be counterproductive. When a follower does not know what to do, he just needs to remember this: obey the orders of the leader.

▶ Not disappointed during marches

A soldier once said, "The greatest tragedy is to retire without fighting a battle." For a soldier who has trained all his life to fight the enemy, it truly is a waste to retire without using any of his knowledge or skills.

In the police too, it is a sad situation, to have retired without creating any positive impact. Whenever Sivanandhan was transferred or took up any posting, he took it up as a challenge.

There are people who run away from troubles. They do not want to face challenges. But to be disappointed by challenges is a waste of a team's skills. A team must be ready to march ahead and not look back. It should take the first step and attack.

The real test of teamwork is during troubled times. In the *Mahabharata*, Arjuna was in midst of the battlefield when he developed cold feet and said he could not fight his family and friends. It required psychological counseling by Shri Krishna in the form of the *Bhagawad Gita* to bring him back to his senses and get ready for war.

When the time for battle comes, do not apply for leave on health or other pretexts. When the call comes, you have to get out of your comfort zone, take up your weapons, pray to God to give you the strength, stand erect and wait for orders.

Then, as the leader instructs, march ahead and give it your best shot. Do not turn back until the battle is won. As the famous saying goes, "Ours is not to make reply, ours is not to reason why, ours is but to do and die."

▶ Able to face challenges

Entering the battlefield does not mean winning the battle. As you get in, you will find many challenges to overcome.

Therefore, the team has to develop the ability to face those challenges.

The team must face the challenges and continue until the goal is achieved. You may start with one strategy. And when you enter the battlefield, you may need to change your strategy to counter the enemy's strategy. This goes on until one of you emerges a winner.

It is physically and mentally tiring to face challenge after challenge. Yet, the leader keeps inspiring the team. At times, he will have to give them a motivational speech; at other times, he will need to lead by example. The highest level of inspiration has to be maintained by the team.

Inspiration is the fuel that keeps a team going during troubled times. Everyone in the team is then ready to sacrifice to win the battle.

During a war, the army is always on the lookout for fresh young recruits. A widow had three sons. The eldest son decided to join as a soldier. He lost his life. The second son, inspired by his elder brother, also wanted to join the army. The neighbors advised the old woman not to give permission. Yet, she did. The second son also lost his life. The youngest son also decided to join the army and went to war with the blessings of his mother. He was also killed.

The neighbors told the old woman, "You have lost all your sons. Did we not tell you not to allow them to join the army? You will regret this for the rest of your life." The old lady replied, "I have just one regret. I do not have a fourth son to send to the war." This is true patriotism; this is ignoring personal benefits for a higher goal.

A good team is comprised of people who set their personal goals aside and focus on what they can contribute to the team's goals.

▶ Experienced in fighting battles

Fighting battles exposes a soldier to real-world challenges. This practical knowledge is more useful than the theory learnt in the classroom. So when the challenge is overcome and the army wins the battle, the soldiers return happier and more powerful than before.

In such a situation, a soldier has been part of the team that made things happen. He has lived the real story. He has real instances to share with others. He can now guide others — show them the path and the pitfalls.

Therefore, a good team should contain senior, experienced members. They can share their experience of fighting previous battles with the young men.

In most government organizations, generally three generations work together. The senior-most generation, 50 years or more in age, is wise and experienced. The second generation comprises people in the mid-30s, who are also experienced but have a long way to go. The third generation is the fresh recruits, who are in their 20s and have yet to understand the real challenges.

A good organization will make sure that the three generations work in sync with each other. The experienced members will share their knowledge and wisdom with the younger ones. And the younger lot will bring fresh ideas and new perspectives to the team.

A typical example is the computer era. The older generation is not comfortable with technology. However, the young, tech-savvy boys and girls in an organization can help the older generation learn these skills.

▶ Skilled in war and weapons

No war can be fought without weapons. Yet, the man behind the machine is more important than the machine. A good team needs to have a mix of strategy and resources. A leader has to ensure that both are in place.

A team may have the required weapons without knowing how to use them. In this case, the leader has to ensure that the team is given adequate training.

For example, many organizations purchase the latest computers, but their old employees do not use them, due to fear of technology, complacency, reluctance to leave their comfort zone or unwillingness to learn. In this case, the organization's leaders must find a way around these barriers and help employees to learn new skills.

Sometimes, a team's resources are not used optimally. For example, most mobile phones today have a plethora of functions, but a study has revealed that almost 90% of these applications are not used by users. Similarly, a simple program like Microsoft Excel can be used for programming but is used most often as a calculator.

While we may not use all the applications on the mobile phone or computer, at least some of them should be used at the optimum level.

Those who are skilled in war, meaning those who are tactful, should document their ideas and share them with others. Some people have the ability or knack to get to the heart of the matter immediately. If a person in a team has such a skill, he should share it with others and help the team develop that skill.

A good team is one that understands the problem immediately and finds quick solutions.

In the police force, for example, investigating cases is teamwork, where the team uses the help of its various members and experts to nab the culprit quickly.

▶ Has no separate self-interest

All members of the team should be connected to the team's vision. Even if one person is selfish, it can destroy the whole plan. One rotten apple can ruin the whole basket.

A leader should have the ability to pick that rotten apple and eliminate it from the system before it can cause severe damage. In the movie *Company*, you will see an instance of this. The actor, Mohanlal plays the role of Sivanandhan, the police officer. In the film, an inspector in his core team is an informer to the underworld. He nabs the culprit through phone tapping and eliminates the rotten apple of the team.

One of the reasons for corruption, whether in government or in business organizations, is that men in power forget their responsibilities and misuse the power given to them for selfish ends. They start taking bribes. If the leader starts taking bribes, it is easy for his team members to follow.

Good teams are formed by people who have the attitude of service to others, also called *Seva Bhav*. If we can bring that back in our generation, the future of our nation will be brighter, and history will look upon us with pride and enthusiasm.

PART C

LEADERSHIP IN ACTION

Inspiring Your Team

Coming together is a beginning.
Keeping together is progress.
Working together is success.

HENRY FORD

SIVANANDHAN'S CAREER CLEARLY illustrates that the key to success is having an effective team. The leader has to create that team. A person may start as a one-man army, but success comes from teamwork.

When you look at a good team, you will find there is a great leader leading from the front. In Sivanandhan's life too, his success was due to his seniors who allowed him to perform the task in hand and encouraged him to do better.

He proactively utilized the media and received wide media coverage during his career. Yet, none of his seniors felt that he was hogging the limelight. They were his role models, as he was a role model for his subordinates.

Creating a good team is important for a leader. When we study history, we find that good leaders had great teams. Akbar had the *Navratnas*, the nine gems in his team, his think-tank. It consisted of experts in various fields like Birbal, the clever minister and Tansen, the well-known singer.

Shivaji had a good team of ministers too – they were called the *Ashta-adhyaksha*. The eight ministers of his core team were dedicated to his cause. These team members were an important part of the work that Shivaji did.

Similarly, Sivanandhan too had his dedicated team members who were instrumental in getting results. Here's how his team and team-building skills embody Chanakya's description of a good team.

▶ Obedient

Creating a *Dand* or army is like bringing up a group of children with love, care and attention. Each child is different and has to be handled in a different way. Like the coach of a sports team, the leader has to select the players carefully. Next, he has to hit the ground and give them training. There should be good and continuous practice.

When required, a little bit of punishment also has to be given. Make sure the team members do not take things for granted. Discipline is required so that the work in hand is taken seriously. Finally, when the time comes, all of them should be focused on the goal to be achieved as one strong unit.

Sivanandhan knew that it was good to have obedient people in his team. If he found indiscipline, he knew that obedience could be achieved through various methods, including punishments.

Retired Assistant Commissioner of Police, Dashrath Avhad, who worked with Sivanandhan, has this to say about the latter's team-building skills, "As a leader, he forgave mistakes and gave his team of officers time to rectify their mistakes. He also encouraged them. One of his rules was very clear. He rarely spoke to the officer or commented on his report file when he was angry. He waited for some time to pass and for him to cool down and then wrote his comments. None of his actions were on the spur of the moment. He was very balanced in his approach.

"Welfare of the police force was also one of his top priorities. He respected the police officer, irrespective of the designation. He particularly took care of the constables, the lowest rung in the force and often the most neglected lot. Wherever he was posted, he would strive for the welfare of the constables. He ensured that their children got good education and motivated them to study and make progress."

Thus, obedience can also be achieved through encouragement and taking care of your team's welfare.

▶ Not disappointed during marches

In a government department such as the police, where transfers are part of the job, you work with different teams. Each team is unique and has its strengths and weaknesses. Often, you do not get to select the team you will lead. Either you are imposed upon them as a leader, or they are imposed upon you as a team.

Even then, Sivanandhan was always on the lookout for officers to build his core team. The qualities he searched for were integrity coupled with performance. It is a rare combination indeed. There are people, who are honest, but their honesty becomes a bottleneck and they do not produce results. There are others who are result-oriented but achieve their goals by unethical means.

This was Sivanandhan's special skill — to identify such dedicated officers who would readily take up the mantle when it was time for action.

▶ Experienced in fighting battles

The most important instance of brilliant teamwork is the eradication of the underworld nexus during his posting as Jt CP (crime) in Mumbai. A good team needs to have excellent coordination, communication and also obedience to the leader.

Coordination is important in teams. In the case of police, it can be a matter of life and death. Even if one person makes a mistake, the whole team can get affected. It is like making a pyramid from a pack of cards. One builds the pyramid slowly and carefully. Even if one of the cards is placed wrongly, the whole pyramid can come down in a split second.

In the same manner, when a police team is working, extreme coordination among the members is essential.

Communication is essential among team members and also with the team leader. In the thick of action, the leader acts like the control tower. He gathers information from the team members, analyzes the situation and takes quick decisions. At times, the team members may also need to take decisions.

One more issue a team can face is egos of the various members. To keep a check on the same and make sure the team stands united is not an easy task.

Purely thanks to perfect teamwork, the team got seven President's medals for Meritorious Service and Sivanandhan was awarded a President's medal for Distinguished Service. Of all the President's medals awarded to the Mumbai police that year, only one medal went to another team. It was not Sivanandhan's individual performance that got the awards; his entire team was a winner.

This shows Sivanandhan's team was now experienced in fighting many wars with the underworld. Having fought many battles, they were able to restore peace.

▶ Skilled in wars and weapons

Sivanandhan used various means to improve the skills of the police force. He organized four seminars after the Mumbai terror attack to provide intellectual inputs to his team.

Focusing on the theme "Preparedness to Fight against Terrorism", these seminars brought together eminent experts. Some of these were APJ Abdul Kalam – former president of India, K Shankaranarayanan – Governor of Maharashtra, MK Narayanan – Intelligence Bureau chief, RR Patil – Home Minister of Maharashtra, Julio Ribeiro – one of the most respected top cops who was instrumental in the crackdown on Sikh militants during the '80s as DGP of Punjab police, AN Roy – DGP of Maharashtra Police, Shyamal Dutta – Former Governor of Nagaland, Commodore Udaya Bhaskar – a reputed security analyst, Anil Kakodkar – Chairman of Atomic Energy Commission of India, Dr Raghunath Anant Mashelkar – Director General of the Council of Scientific and Industrial Research (CSIR) and advisor to the prime minister, MJ Akbar – one of India's most distinguished journalists, Kumar Ketkar – editor of *Loksatta*, a popular Marathi newspaper, Sundeep Waslekar – an advisor to various governments across the globe, Gopalaswami Parthasarathy – a distinguished diplomat, Bahukutumbai Raman – former head of the counterterrorism wing of India's Research and Analysis Wing (R&AW), KPS Gill – former DGP of Punjab, Pravin Swami – associate editor of *The Hindu*, and Dr Ashok Bhan, former DGP of Jammu and Kashmir.

These experts spoke on topics such as steps to preempt terrorism, timely and tactical intelligence to win the war against terrorism, thinking one step ahead of the terrorists and the corporatization of terror.

These seminars gave the attending police officers different perspectives of the same subject. Sharp minds sharing their experiences is the best training one can give to his team.

Another way of skill-building is to encourage team members to read books. As we have seen in previous chapters, Sivanandhan started many libraries in various police offices. Thousands of books on diverse subjects, such as management, health, leadership, arts and literature, were purchased and distributed among the policemen to encourage the reading habit. Police officers, who earlier did not get the time to read because of their busy schedules, now had easier access to books as they were available in the police offices itself.

To build skills for war in a team, training is very important. Sivanandhan achieved this by creating training centers.

Sivanandhan paid special attention to organizing regular training programs for team building. Setting up new, world-class training centers was a part of his passion and work.

▶ **Has no separate self-interest**

The Mumbai terror attack shook the whole world. Though the Mumbai Police got into action rapidly, it was not equipped for a war-like situation. As a result, many policemen, including senior officers, lost their lives, and it took hours and days to bring down the terrorists.

This shows that the Mumbai Police, even though it was not ready, did not wait to get into action. There was no separate self-interest. Many lost their lives too in the process.

▶ **Able to face challenges**

One of the major takeaways from this experience was that precious hours are lost in the time taken for the Army and the National Security Guards (NSG) to arrive into the city.

Organizing training programs is good, but the best way to establish continuous training as a system is to set up training institutions. Apart from the Maharashtra Intelligence Academy and other training centers at various points in his career, Sivanandhan was instrumental in setting up Force 1 after the Mumbai terror attack.

Force 1 is an elite commando force, a specialized counter-terrorism unit to guard Mumbai. It was formed under the supervision of Sivanandhan by the Government of Maharashtra.

It is on the lines of the NSG with headquarters in Mumbai. Force 1 was commissioned on 24 November, 2009.

The commandos of Force 1 are given the best training. They are trained in the use of sophisticated arms and explosives, which can be used in rapid shooting. To get the best of world-class training, two months of basic training was given by Israeli specialists.

In parallel, the central government also set up a regional hub of NSG in Mumbai. However, Force 1 is expected to be part of the initial response to any terror strike in Mumbai.

Force 1 takes only 15 minutes to respond to a terror strike. Its speed and swiftness to action is its strength.

To create an institution like Force 1 in a short period of time was not easy. But Sivanandhan had the ability to put up with the troubles that came on the way and finally produce results.

The Maharashtra Intelligence Academy was set up in 2009 in Pune. The objective was to train police officers in intelligence gathering, especially regarding terrorist networks and activities. After a year-long training, these officers would then be recruited as Intelligence Officers to the State Intelligence Department (SID).

These officers will remain in the intelligence force for 25-30 years and periodic and refresher courses will be given to upgrade their skills. It has been a very successful model.

Furthermore, for good teams to be created, the leader needs to inspire and motivate them. This can happen only if the team expends efforts beyond what is required by its scope of work. It is said that if one has to win a game on the field, it depends on the efforts put off the field.

Sivanandhan organized a lot of activities to encourage bonding in the police force.

One such mega event was the 100 years of Maharashtra Police Games in 2006. The first Police Games were held in 1906; when Sivanandhan realized this, he saw a golden opportunity to bring all the policemen together through a spirit of competition and sportsmanship.

The centenary year of the Maharashtra Police Games was a hugely successful event that enthused the whole police force.

Therefore, through these events, he ensured inclusive growth in the team. One of Sivanandhan's hobbies is to organize events. He used his event management skills to bring in various sportsmen, Bollywood stars and celebrities to participate and entertain the police force. These included Sachin Tendulkar, Aamir Khan and other top actors.

Many policemen have unique talents which they never get an opportunity to display in their strenuous work schedules. He encouraged his team members to participate in stage shows like dance and drama. During the Kala Ghoda festival of Mumbai, the police had put up a special stall, where policemen displayed their painting and art skills.

One final but important quality of a leader is to give credit to the team members. Share your success with the people.

When a problem comes to you, take the responsibility. When you achieve success, you give the credit to your team members. Thus, they are inspired to work with enthusiasm.

During his three-year tenure as Deputy Inspector General of Police, Nagpur range, he was ably assisted by dedicated and brilliant superintendents in the police in all the six districts. Sivanandhan had delegated all his financial powers to them. Since these areas were Naxal-infested, taking care of security and building morale in the force were of paramount importance.

Sivanandhan impressed the then Addl Chief Secretary (Home), and through an empowered committee, got financial sanctions for huge amounts of money to reform all the police stations, which were temporary sheds made out of tin sheets. These structures had flimsy compound walls and would frequently be attacked by Naxals. Sivanandhan undertook the major task of revamping all the compound walls to make them so strong that the Naxals would never dare attack again. He also constructed pucca (permanent and strong) structures inside the fortified walls so that his men within felt safe. Not a single attack took place after that.

He also visited them frequently to mingle with them and boost their morale. The parliamentary and the state legislature elections took place without any untoward incident, in spite of the Naxal call for a ban and the neighboring state of Andhra Pradesh witnessing a lot of violence.

Sivanandhan had a medical examination conducted for the commandos in an orthopedic hospital and proved that the shoes worn by the personnel, which were issued by the government, were detrimental to their bones. He got special shoes custom-made for jungle operations. He also canvassed with the government and got their daily refreshment allowance doubled, simultaneously encouraging the government to build two private housing colonies for the policemen. One of these is located near Gadchiroli and the other is in Chandrapur.

Two police schools built by Sivanandhan in Chandrapur and Gadchiroli towns are still running very well. He arranged to build proper guest houses in each district headquarters for the police officers and men to stay during their visits. During his tenure as DGP of the state, Sivanandhan succeeded in arranging for a wet lease of Pawan Hans helicopters, so that all men wounded in the Naxal ambushes could be evacuated immediately to Nagpur for medical treatment. Many lives have been saved so far due to this initiative.

Any leader should develop three qualities – an open mind to receive new ideas from his team, a broad shoulder to take responsibilities of the team and a large heart to accept the weaknesses of the team members.

When the team finally wins the game, celebrating success is also required.

Appreciate the hard work and commitment of each team member. Each of them has given personal sacrifices to reach the goal. Each of them has played a small role in reaching the big goal. Even nuts and bolts are required for a big machine to produce the required goods.

Give credit to the last man. Even those who may not have played the game, but have been cheering in the stands, are required to win the game. Even they are part of the success. Therefore, teamwork is all-inclusive. A leader understands this and with the team backing him, confidently proceeds towards the next big game....

The final secret is the *mitra*. The next chapter will focus on how friends help you grow in your career and life.

★   TIPS TO INSPIRE YOUR TEAM   ★

1. Identify your people: Look for people who are honest and achieve results.

2. Go beyond work: Teamwork is inspiring people beyond the work they do in office.

3. Impart training: Create world-class institutions and training programs.

4. Encourage people: Organize events, including sports and entertainment.

5. Give credit: Share successes with your team.

The Leader in Me

Notes

Chapter 7

Mitra

ALLY/CONSULTANT

Swami	the king
Amatya	the minister
Janpada	the country
Durg	the fortified city
Kosha	the treasury
Dand	the army
Mitra	**the ally**

THE SEVENTH SECRET

Mitra: The Ally or Consultant

MITRA, A WORD commonly used in all Indian languages, means a friend, buddy, colleague or partner. It forms the last pillar of Chanakya's Seven Pillars model.

Even the most powerful king requires a *mitra*, for the friend is with you through thick and thin, in good times and bad.

He is the friend, philosopher and guide. You can depend upon him and he is true to you. He can hold up a mirror and show you what is real.

He can tell you when your breath smells bad, without you feeling offended. He is the lighthouse that shows you the way. He is the consultant who offers you the right advice at the right time.

This seventh secret can change the dynamics of any game. A friend can make or break you completely.

The story of the *Mahabharata* illustrates the importance of choosing the right advisor at the right time. Before the war at Kurukshetra was to begin, the Pandavas and the Kauravas were seeking allies. Both wanted Krishna on their side. Therefore, Arjuna on behalf of the Pandavas, and Duryodhana representing the Kauravas went to meet Krishna.

Krishna was asleep when they arrived, so they decided to wait till he woke up. Arjuna waited near Krishna's feet, while Duryodhana sat beside his head.

When Krishna woke up, he asked them the purpose of their visit. Both requested Krishna for an alliance in the forthcoming war against each other. Krishna could not accept one's request and refuse the other, for he was a cousin to both of them.

The quick-witted Krishna replied, "I will support both of you. On one side will be my entire army of experienced warriors, fully armed. And on the other side will be myself, but I will be unarmed and will not fight in the war. Each of you can choose which you want."

Krishna added, "Since I saw Arjuna first when I woke up and he is younger to you, Duryodhana, I will give him the opportunity to choose first."

Arjuna unhesitatingly chose Krishna. Duryodhana, who was worried that Arjuna might choose Krishna's powerful army, was now secretly delighted. He thought that with Krishna's army on his side, he could not lose the war; and that Arjuna had made a wrong choice by choosing only Krishna who would not fight.

However, the Pandavas won the war due to Krishna's strategic advice at every turn. As Arjuna's charioteer, Krishna was always with them, guiding them slowly towards success.

Such is the power of choosing the right advisor. An intelligent person is the biggest asset of any team or organization.

Successful companies understand the value of good advisors. Therefore, they have advisory panels which guide them from time to time.

A student wanted to learn to play the flute. He had two choices — a mediocre teacher who would charge a lower fee, and a very good teacher whose fee the student could not afford. However, he still wanted to get the best possible choice. An expert's services may be costly, but he can help you reach the goal faster.

You will commit fewer mistakes if you have the best advisor on your side.

Therefore, the student went to the best teacher and explained his deep desire to learn the flute from him. He also explained that he would not be able to pay the high fees, but was willing to offer services in kind as compensation.

The teacher laughed, "The high fee is just to filter the students who come to me. I am happy there is a burning desire to learn in you. Come from tomorrow; you don't have to pay any fee."

A good teacher also requires a good student. In the same way, a good advisor requires a person who would understand and implement the advice. So, if you are ready to take advice, listen to only the best. It will then be a win-win situation for you and your advisor.

A friend is ready to help you in crises. Even the two World Wars are the stories of group of allies.

If you have seen the television game show *Kaun Banega Crorepati* or *Who Wants to Be a Millionaire*, you will know that one of the "lifelines" for the player is "Phone a friend". The friend comes to the player's rescue when the player is stuck. This is the best and most powerful tool one can apply.

So, when the going gets tough, take the help of *mitras*.

Some people hesitate or feel belittled if they have to ask for help. This is disaster. There should not be any ego connected to reaching out to a friend. No one is perfect. Therefore, asking a friend for help can save a lot of trouble. Make use of friends and let friends use you. Friendship is always a win-win situation for both parties. It is mutual give and take.

In friendship, happiness is shared and sorrows are divided.

How does one develop friends? You must have a friendly nature. You should genuinely want to make friends, rather than just use other people for your benefit. You should also be open-minded towards people who come into your life.

A leader is open-minded, and therefore, ready to learn from everyone.

Chanakya advised leaders to learn from everyone, including children. Children may not have knowledge and experience, but they are pure, open-minded and truthful. They sometimes give insights that many adults overlook. Their opinions are not colored by selfish desires. Therefore, to listen to children is to listen to the voice of God.

Once, a king wanted the world's most beautiful clothes to be made for him. The tailor missed the deadline and showed the king an imaginary outfit, describing it as his masterpiece. The king could not see anything, but did not want to be considered a fool for not being able to see the outfit. The tailor pretended to dress the king in the outfit, though in reality, the king had not worn anything.

The king went in a procession to display his new clothes. All the citizens on the streets did not want to get punished for pointing out the truth, so they heaped praises on the king's clothes.

Suddenly, a child on the street started laughing and shouting, "The king is naked." Everyone was shocked and expected the king to punish the little one.

Yet, that statement brought the king to his senses. He realized his mistake and the fool he had made of himself in his desire for self-glorification. Instead of punishing the child, he appreciated the child for being the only honest person in his whole kingdom.

Thus, even a child can be your ally, giving you wisdom and common sense. But then, as Voltaire said, "Common sense is not so common."

That is why everyone requires a friend, who can be a guide, consultant and advisor.

In the *Arthashastra*, various sutras or verses describe the qualities of good consultants and a leader's need for good consultants and advisors.

In Book 1, Chapter 15, Verses 2, 35 and 40 of the *Arthashastra*, Chanakya says,

"All undertakings should be preceded by consultation. Holding a consultation with only one, he may not be able to reach a decision in difficult matters. With more councilors, it is difficult to reach decisions and maintain secrecy."

A king is as good or bad as his advisors. Therefore, the leader has to be selective in his choice of advisors and the advice he gets, because the decisions he takes based on the advice can make or break a nation.

Remember the story in the *Ramayana* when Kaikayee was wrongly advised by Manthara and the crown prince was exiled on the day of the crowning ceremony. Kaikayee herself was happy about Rama becoming the king, but wrong advice from her advisor had far-reaching implications for the kingdom.

Therefore, Chanakya's warning must be heeded.

Let us explore this verse further.

▶ All undertakings

The important word is "all". All activities, small or big, should be preceded by consultation. Always consult others before you start any project or assignment. Thus, you will think along with others and not alone.

Say, you want to buy new office. Ask a consultant and a few other people and then start. You will be able to learn more about the advantages and disadvantages of the office space you are considering. Thus, it will be easier to take a decision.

▶ Holding a consultation with only one

Having a single advisor will make you too dependent on that person. He may guide you, but there is also the danger that he may misguide you. Take a second opinion.

When a doctor says a particular condition is not curable, do not get depressed and stop there; try another doctor. In many medical cases, a second opinion has helped cure diseases that were considered incurable by the first doctor.

The second doctor can often bring in a fresh perspective, which helps to cure the patient. In short, Chanakya says, never be dependent on any one person.

Good organizations have more than one consultant, as well as more than one vendor and supplier. This is a way of spreading risks. Especially when an organization is faced with complex issues, it will require the inputs of more than one consultant.

A management consultant explains, "If your business is completely dependent on one client, you will have to go as per the whims and fancies of that client. The client can control your pricing and finances, and without your knowledge, it will become a one-sided game. Therefore, the best strategy is to have at least five clients, that is, 20% dependency on each client."

However, the reverse is also true. If you have too many advisors and keep taking each one's suggestions, you will get confused and will find it difficult to take a decision.

There is this story of a farmer and his son, who purchased a donkey. They were returning home with their purchase. A passerby suggested, "Why don't one of you sit on the donkey? That way, you can save your energy." The father sat on the donkey and the son walked alongside.

Further down the road, another passerby commented, "Look at the father. He is comfortably sitting on the donkey and is making his son walk in the heat." The father felt guilty and asked the son to take his place.

They had gone some distance when they met another passerby. "Look at the son," said the passerby. "He does not know his duty towards his father. Our culture asks the son to work for his parents' comfort." The father and son were confused now. Finally, they both decided to sit on the donkey.

As they were nearing home, a passerby commented, "What a tragedy! The poor donkey has to carry the weight of these two cruel men. Nobody thinks about the mute donkey."

The father and son considered this and decided to carry the donkey on their shoulders.

When they reached home, the farmer's wife commented, "What a useless family I have! Could you not just walk home with the donkey? Why are you carrying it on your shoulders?"

"That is exactly how we started the journey!" said the father and son.

Thus, it is foolish to take everyone's advice. There is a difference between advice and opinion. Opinion is a personal matter, but advice must be taken only from mature and intelligent people. Comments are not advice. Advice is given after seriously thinking through issues.

When you go to someone for advice, you will have to explain your problem clearly to the person concerned. If you do that with a hundred people, your problem will be known to the whole world and it will no more be a secret.

So, what is the solution?

In the *Arthashastra*, Book 1, Chapter 15, Verses 20-21, Chanakya says,

"Therefore sit and counsel with those who are mature in intellect."

We should therefore choose our consultants very carefully.

▶ Mature in intellect

It is very important for a consultant to be mature in "intellect". The consultant can be young in age, yet mature in that particular field. This is often seen in the police force.

For example, in the case of cyber crimes, the experts are generally young police officers. They understand the issues better than most senior officers.

▶ Sit and counsel

Sitting here is symbolic. The term *Upanishad* means sitting below a spiritual master and listening to his wisdom. Similarly, when you are sitting with a mature and intelligent person, you should be receptive like a good student in class.

Also, do not just listen to your advisor as if he were delivering a sermon. Discuss the problem with him; ask him questions to obtain clarity on the issues concerned.

The time taken out for consultation is a very serious affair. It is not just a casual meeting. It means business for both parties.

Chanakya goes to the extent of saying that when one is getting counsel, there should not be any disturbance. Consultation requires a secluded space. Therefore, make sure your mobile phone is switched off; you do not browse the internet and are not distracted by other, unrelated issues during a consultation.

Kings were instructed to have a panel of advisors — the council of ministers — with whom they would spend time daily to discuss the matters of the state.

Akbar had the *Navratnas*, the nine jewels, as he called them. These nine experts were his personal counselors. They were from different fields. Therefore, he could get different perspectives on each issue.

Shivaji Maharaj had *Ashta-Pradhan*, eight heads of various departments. These were his core team members and all strategies and action plans were made with their help.

Why think alone when there are other experts who can think with you?

You will often find businessmen, who are not very qualified, but successfully run multinational companies. The secret of such a businessman's success is that his team comprises highly educated and globally experienced people. They are paid well and taken care of, and in return, they bring their experience and expertise to the company.

Make sure to pay your advisors very well. Consultants cannot be valued in terms of money. They are an asset by themselves. In a way, all of a consultant's advice is free, and on the other hand, all of it is priceless. You cannot bargain or negotiate for good advice. Consulting firms that do this devalue their consultants.

One of the strengths of Duryodhana was that he took excellent care of his team. In the Kurukshetra war, the best warriors of that generation – Bheeshma, Dronacharya, Kripacharya and Karna – were with the Kauravas.

Duryodhana took good care of them. When Karna was insulted, Duryodhana gave a part of his kingdom to him. He made Karna a king from nothing.

Is that not a quality that we should learn from Duryodhana?

He kept his team members and advisors happy and satisfied. So, they were with him during the war, despite knowing Duryodhana was in the wrong. They showered him with valuable advice to take the right path. Duryodhana may not have followed their advice, yet all the great men stuck with him till the end of their lives.

If you take care of your consultants, they will take care of you. In most organizations, the consultant becomes a part of the family and stays with the organization forever. He truly becomes the *mitra*, the true friend who will be with you till the last breath.

In a war, a soldier returned safely from the enemy camp. However, he found out that his friend was missing and insisted on going back into enemy territory. His commander said, "It is meaningless to go back and give up your life." But the soldier, for once, did not pay heed.

When he came back, he was riddled with bullets but brought his dead friend on his shoulder. The commander said, "I had lost one soldier; I am now going to lose two. Did it make any sense for you to go back?"

The soldier said, "I found my friend lying in the enemy camp nearly dead. When I reached him, he said, 'I knew you would come.'

"Sir, it did make sense for me to listen to those last words, because I could give up my life, but not my friendship." And he died.

ACCORDING TO CHANAKYA

Qualities of a Good Ally

LEADERS CANNOT WALK the path alone. Like anyone else, they too require companions. There is a saying, "It is lonely at the top," but you can make friends with others who are at the top.

Seek friends lifelong. Friendship is about companionship. It is the shoulder you can lean upon when you feel low.

Look at other leaders, not necessarily those from your field. You can learn from various leadership styles.

Harsha Bhogle, the famous cricket commentator, once said, "What do cricketers know if they know only about cricket!"

This is a profound statement. A cricketer can learn from a swimmer, a golfer, a tennis player or a football player. The sport may be different, but he can learn from different sportspersons. Champions learn from others champions. Winners learn from other winners. Leaders learn from other leaders.

Leaders also evolve to the next level. They want to grow; to learn, unlearn and relearn. They want to share their knowledge and experience.

Once you are in a leadership position, it becomes fun. It becomes a hobby and a game. And you require friends to play games. You require like-minded people. Then, life is not just easy, but a continuous learning process.

Chanakya says, while choosing your allies, you should look for some qualities. The qualities of a good ally given in the *Arthashastra* (Book 6, Chapter 1, Verse 12) are:

- Alliance from the days of your father/grandfather
- Greatness
- Constancy
- Self-control
- No separate self-interest
- Ability to mobilize quickly

One day, a child joined a new school. On his first day, the child was quiet and reserved and came home sad and depressed.

His mother asked, "Did you not like the school? Did you not make any new friends today?"

The boy replied, "The school is very good. The teachers are nice. All the other children came and spoke to me."

"Then what is the problem? Why are you sad?" asked the mother.

"My problem is, I could not decide who is a good friend and who is not."

Most of us are like this child in a new school. No one can decide in the very first instance who a good friend is. But you still have to take the first step. Begin by being friendly to others. In the long run, some friends go out of your life and some stay back as lifelong friends.

There are some universal qualities you can consider when you choose your friends for life.

▶ Alliance from the days of your father/grandfather

This refers to family friends whom you have known for two or three generations. Many friendships come to you unasked. For instance, your father and the friend's father have known each other for a long time; they are regular visitors to your house and you visit their house regularly.

The families know each other very well and have supported each other in difficult times. You have heard stories about the friendship of your parents. One learns the value of friendship in such an environment.

Such family friendships could also be built over three generations – the grandfather's generation, your father's generation and then your generation. This is symbolic, yet shows how deep the friendship has grown.

In many cases, marriages take place between families that have been friends for generations. The children feel comfortable as they have known each other since childhood. It is like sending the child from one home to another. Since there is perfect tuning among the families, it is easy to adjust.

The longer you know a friend, the better your rapport. Both know each other's strengths and weaknesses, both know how the other person thinks. If you were to start a business venture, which of these would you choose as a partner: a friend whom you have known for over thirty years or a person whom you have recently met? You would choose the former, because of your understanding with each other, built over the years you have spent together.

▶ Greatness

When two people become partners, it is important to respect each other. No two people can think alike; therefore, each person's focus should be to discover the strengths of the other partner. Both partners' strengths should be complementary. Then, it becomes a self-supporting relationship.

In business houses, we find that different partners come with different strengths. If one partner is good at finance, another's strength is marketing, while the third is good at operations.

Your friend should be "great" means that he or she should have qualities that you admire, that you wish to possess.

In life, you will make good and bad friends. A person is known by the kind of friends he has. Good friends can make you, while bad friends can destroy you. Therefore, it is important to have good and "great" friends.

Good friendship is called *Sat-sang* in Sanskrit. It is the company of good, noble and spiritual people. Bad friendship is called *Ku-sang,* the company of evil or bad people.

It is the prime duty of parents to ensure that their children are always in good company.

Sometimes, an average person also becomes great by being in the company of the great. He imbibes noble virtues from his friends and progresses in life.

It is like a piece of iron in the company of a strong magnet. In time, the iron piece imbibes the qualities of the magnet and starts attracting other iron pieces.

On the other hand, a person may be as pure as milk, but when a drop of lemon spills into the milk, irreversible damage can be done. The case of chain smokers and drug addicts is an indication of the consequences of bad company.

Once a devotee was praying and the Lord appeared to grant him a boon. The devotee said, "Oh Lord, bless me that I am always in the company of noble and good-hearted souls." There cannot be any greater boon than that.

▶ Constancy

Everyone wants to associate with successful people. However, very few people support you during the struggle for success. In success, friends know you; and in failure, you know who your friends are.

Therefore, Chanakya points out that the quality of a good friend is to be constant — in times of struggle, failure and also success.

There is a Marathi saying, "*Kama purta mama*," meaning you become a relative only when the need arises. After the work is done, you forget the person. Such friends are like parasites.

Good friends are for all seasons. They stay by you constantly. They love you unconditionally. These friends are the real asset in your life.

Remember what a great saint said, "Money never makes you rich. It is friends who make you rich. Money comes and goes. But good friends stay with you forever."

Leaders need to understand who their real friends are.

Good times or bad times may come and go, but friendship remains forever. The secret of success for every leader lies in the number of his real friends. This is the asset the leader has to develop during his lifetime. In certain communities, the success of a man is measured by the number of people who attend his funeral.

▶ Self-control

This is another test to find out if you have the right friend on your side. He should have self-control. A person who keeps his mind and senses under control can never go wrong. This person will never cross the limit.

He is disciplined, well-mannered and well-behaved. He has a balanced view and does not lose his cool in any situation. Such a person is strong from within.

He controls his thoughts, speech and actions when required. He is not impulsive. He thinks through the consequences before he acts.

Such a friend is a controlled spender too. He is not a miser; yet he will never show off, just because he has the capacity to spend. He never gambles. His purchases are not impulsive. He is not attracted by the lure of credit cards and spends only where needed. He is classy but not flashy.

Being in the company of such a person will also help you develop self-control.

He is surrounded by goodness and attracts goodness. He is an inspiration. He speaks words of wisdom. He knows the difference between right and wrong. He is a thinker and also a doer. He is humility personified.

Wouldn't you like to make such a person your friend, philosopher and guide? With such a friend, your life would be complete and fulfilled.

▶ No separate self-interest

A true *mitra* never thinks of his benefit alone. He thinks win-win. He makes sure that all of you succeed together. There is no separate or individual interest for him in any project or assignment.

For instance, Sivanandhan upheld the value of benefit to society during his police career. At the end of his career, he counts the goodwill and the benefits accrued to society as his biggest assets.

You may also know many such friends who work selflessly towards the welfare of the society and nation. Such people pray for the benefit of mankind. They are the noble ones.

On the other hand, a friend who always thinks only of his personal benefits will lose all his existing friends and will be lonely towards the end.

Friendship can exist not only among individuals, but also among organizations. They come together and create a win-win situation for each other. They focus on everyone's benefit rather than individual benefit.

For example, mobile operators today share the same transmission towers. Instead of spending more on installing additional towers, they have entered a mutually beneficial arrangement to share each other's towers.

Many international organizations, and even the police force, have exchange programs. They mutually exchange employees for participation in training programs. This helps to share knowledge and experience among organizations working in different countries, which helps both organizations to be proactive and more alert towards future events and calamities.

Some organizations also conduct research together. They bring out unique products and services, for which they own joint intellectual property rights (IPR), and share the resultant financial successes.

The concept of associations is similar. Business groups come together to form associations. Individual companies may have lower bargaining power, but together, they work on common problems and protest against government policies that may be harmful to their industry.

Business networks are powerful places where people come together for their mutual interests. There is no separate interest for anyone.

The true strength of friends lies in collaboration, not competition.

Dr Abdul Kalam said, "In the past, leadership style was about competition. Today, it is about collaboration."

Come together, collaborate and think win-win. It is a surefire formula for success.

▶ Ability to mobilize quickly

A good associate will be able to come to your aid immediately. His is the emergency number you can dial without thinking twice.

A true friend will know when you need him, even when you do not tell him. He is mentally attuned to your needs.

A couple married for many years also has that mental connection. They are tuned to each other such that words are not needed for communication.

In troubled times, such friends can be mobilized quickly.

Imagine your house is on fire. You may panic and not be able to think straight. But a true friend will come as soon as you call him and will quickly mobilize the action required, such as calling the fire engine or calling up other friends.

Such brilliant friends are a moral support.

The above six qualities of a *mitra* help us to find good and true friends. You should also make sure to develop these qualities and become a good friend yourself.

Discover the good friend inside you.

PART C

LEADERSHIP IN ACTION

Working Together with Allies and Friends

I would rather walk with a friend in the dark,
than alone in the light.

HELEN KELLER

WHEN SIVANANDHAN WAS a senior police officer, naturally, the power of his position got him a lot of connections. However, the trick was not to just use the influence but make friends forever.

Some friends come into your life due to professional reasons; others due to some need of theirs and we also approach and network with others for some self-interests. Whatever be the starting point, one should not cut off a friendship after the objective is fulfilled. This is where we build relationships beyond reasons.

So long as the friendship exists for a reason, it will not have depth. But, Sivanandhan has maintained his contacts and networks even after his retirement.

When Radhakrishnan Pillai met Sivanandhan, he had only six months to retire. I have known him more after his days as a top cop in uniform. What amazed me was that he commanded the same respect post-retirement.

While interviewing him for this book, I came to know that the network he created was an important contributor to his successful career. Let us look at some important aspects of how he effectively used his *mitras* for success.

Your network will give you a lot of information about what is happening. As a leader in the police force, it was important to not just gather information, but also make sure that the flow of information was regular and actions were taken accordingly.

When a person is in a position of authority, information comes to him unasked. For example, if you are the head of a department in a university, you will automatically get information about your field on your table every day. You will get invitations for seminars, best research journals, occasions to attend meetings with other experts in the field and so on.

However, a good leader goes one step ahead in his network. He does not just wait for information to come to him. He proactively seeks out information.

Sivanandhan was a leader of the police force. His subordinates knew the ground reality and were masters in their respective fields. So, he had a system of daily meetings, where he discussed issues of concern with his subordinates, listened to others and took decisions to be implemented.

The daily meetings, analysis and decisions were part of his daily routine throughout his career. Meeting with key members of the team face to face helps in resolving confusions.

Even in the corporate world, we find the same system being used effectively. Daily meetings have ensured good leadership. Sales have increased, teamwork has become strong and financial control is also guaranteed. In the hotel industry, the general manager of the hotel has a daily morning meeting. He checks the room occupancy status, the maintenance problems, the attendance of his staff and any other matters of concern.

During these daily meetings, the leader also gets an opportunity to share his side of the story with his team. This clear two-way communication bridges the gap of miscommunication, which can lead to disaster.

In policing, your network in the form of informers or *khabaris* is a great asset. These informers provide inside information of the various gangs that operate in the city or state. These informers are the key to many landmark breakthroughs.

Information can come to a police leader either from an immediate subordinate, a constable, an informer, or a common man who just walks into your office unasked. The next step is to listen to these with an open mind and analyze the information. Dig deeper and check what is useful to you and make use of the same.

The larger your network of informers, the stronger you are. Have multiple sources of gathering information. Information could also be through newspapers, television or a journalist who knows different aspects of the case.

In this context, Sivanandhan has an interesting insight, "A leader should be like a swan who knows how to differentiate between milk and water, and take the best out of it."

While one can gather multiple pieces of information from various sources, which one will be true and correct? That itself is a challenge. Therefore, the skill required for separating milk and water is required. In our Indian scriptures, this skill is called *Viveka-Buddhi* — the faculty of our intellect to discriminate between right and wrong, good and bad, relevant and irrelevant, needed and useless.

In the *Arthashastra*, this skill of thinking is called *Aanvikshiki*, a method of strategic thinking and analysis.

There is a simple method by which you can analyze contradictory information and find out which is correct:

"Have three information sources, take the average of what each of them say and decide."

So, if you are not sure of a situation, check with three people separately. You will find the reality when one takes the average of the information collected. As Sivanandhan says, "The truth always lies somewhere in between."

Apart from sources of information, one should also keep the company of good advisors. These advisors are more mature and senior to you. They have experience, wisdom and insight. Sivanandhan made sure that he kept learning from his senior cops. From one senior, he learnt the importance of discipline and punctuality; from another, he learnt that dressing well makes one feel positive; from a third, he learnt how to take quick action.

These advisors also come handy when one requires direction and inputs for creating a strategy. After the 26/11 Mumbai terror attack, Sivanandhan arranged seminars to gather wisdom from the best brains of India. This also comes from good networking skills.

Your colleagues and friends in the police community also give you inputs. For example, when Sivanandhan was the Director General of Maharashtra Police, he had friends in other states, who were at similar positions. Some of them were his batchmates; others he had met as part of his work.

One can make use of these contacts. It is like sharing information with each other. So, if a gangster has fled from one state to another, the *mitra* in another state will come handy. One phone call will help to activate the police force in another state and nab the gangster.

In national-level police meetings, one interacts with various other state police officers. One comes to know what is happening elsewhere. During these gatherings, one gets an opportunity to develop new friends. If one is smart, one can maintain these contacts for a lifetime.

Sivanandhan was highly networked among various levels of policemen across the state, nation and the world. These formal and informal networks and communities that he created has always been one of his core strengths.

There are different types of *mitras* one needs to have: those who are part of your group and community, and those who are not part of your group. Sivanandhan had many friends who were not from the police community.

There is a saying, "Birds of a feather flock together." This is natural. But it takes effort to fly with birds that are not of the same feather. Having a lot of friends in the police community would be natural for Sivanandhan, but having good friends in other circles was critical to his success.

His friends included teachers, professors, academicians, doctors, lawyers, engineers, chartered accountants, management consultants, journalists and media experts.

We will see with a few examples how these friends also helped him from time to time.

With his friends in the media and journalism, he launched the first Mumbai Police magazine, *The Mumbai Protector*. This was in association with the New Media group. The magazine, which is available by subscription, is a good way of communicating the initiatives taken by the police to the common man.

The Protector is the only magazine that informs you and also connects you with the cops. It is a world-class magazine that features interviews of top cops and influential people in the society. It has been in circulation for nearly two years and is widely read by the police and the common man.

The New Media group also brings out various books and publications related to police functions, such as the compilation of speeches of the seminars held to combat terrorism.

Sivanandhan's friends in the medical field also helped him take various health initiatives for the police force, such as a complete health check-up of policemen, and printing of booklets that gave health tips and their circulation to each police personnel.

The setting up of the Thane Police Hospital run under the management of Wockhardt group is another example. Here too, the policemen are given financially beneficial health schemes to enable them to obtain world-class medical treatment.

Today, the new terminology in the government is "public management". Sivanandhan had many friends who were experts in the management field. He organized lectures, seminars and workshops of management consultants like (late) Rooshi Kumar Pandya to improve the management skills of the police force.

His networking skills in various business associations also helped him raise funds for many projects. Instead of the government bearing all the costs, friends from the corporate world helped him finance projects such as getting bulletproof jackets, or creating gymnasiums, schools and canteens.

Also, to communicate the message of the police to the common man, he gave hundreds of lectures through organizations like Rotary Clubs, Lions Clubs, Indian merchant chambers, etc.

While working with friends, it is important to look at a win-win situation for both parties. As the police force benefited, so these groups also benefited from their association with the police force. The image of a leader in the police began to change. Approaching the policeman became easy; the walls that divided the people from a policeman began to fall.

A good leader is one who appreciates leaders from other fields. He respects them, learns from them and finally collaborates with them for mutual benefit.

No society can progress without helping each other. For that, leaders of every field should come together and help each other grow.

The relations that you build should last for a lifetime. It should be permanent.

Sivanandhan's networking skills have helped him post-retirement too. From a police leader, he is now a corporate executive. He is the chairman of Securus First, a company that provides security services for large corporations in India and abroad.

The skills that were used to eliminate crime, corruption and economic offences are now being effectively used to guide various organizations towards better security.

Post-retirement, he was called by the government of India, by the National Security Advisor (NSA) under the Prime Minister's office (PMO) to be a member of the special task force for study and recommendations on internal and external security. This special task force was headed by ex-Cabinet Secretary, Shri Naresh Chandra. These projects do not come easily. They come due to your vast experience and goodwill that you have generated over years.

He is also the security advisor to the Reserve Bank of India (RBI), planning strategies against new-age crimes like cyber crimes and electronic theft. He continues to be an advisor to various corporate homes and teaches management and leadership lessons in some of the premier institutions in India and abroad.

There are many bureaucrats who get a cultural shock after they retire from the powerful post they held. For years, they were followed by thousands of men who would be willing to sacrifice their lives at one command. The power that a senior policeman held could send fear waves among people.

Yet, the day one retires, everything is taken away. There is no more command or authority; no further orders can be given. But what stays is the goodwill that you have created, the friends you made along the way. They are real assets that stay with you forever. Furthermore, in the course of working on this book, we got acquainted with each others *Mitras*. Our assets of friends have only grown with time. This is our real asset.

In conclusion, let us see how Chanakya's description of a good *mitra* comes alive in Sivanandhan's case.

▶ Alliance from the days of father/grandfather

Sivanandhan has kept in touch with batchmates of his IPS course and other government departments even after his retirement. Over a period of 35 plus years, these relationships span over generations. Thus, these have become time-tested relationships – allied from the days of father/grandfather.

▶ Greatness

Sivanandhan kept in touch with great people from different fields. If someone is better than you in his field, make sure you respect such people, be it doctors, management consultants, lawyers, or professionals in other government departments. He always associated with great people.

▶ Constancy

The power and seniority of his position gave Sivanandhan the opportunity to meet a lot of new people. However, he used his position to make friends who would be with him forever.

▶ Self-control

In the police force, it is important to exercise self-control. You will get mouthwatering offers like getting a criminal to do some work for a large sum of money. These may come as a friendship deal, but it is important not to get carried away. Sivanandhan's integrity ensured that he was always in control. He has been on the right side of the law and has lived up to his reputation of an honest officer.

▶ No separate self-interest

When Sivanandhan met corporate groups or medical professionals who eventually helped him realize his goals for the police force, he did not look at such possibilities from the perspective of, "What is in it for me?" Instead, his outlook was always to create a win-win situation for the police force and his friends. Thus, not having a separate self-interest helps you create tremendous goodwill.

▶ Ability to mobilize quickly

Whether it was fundraising, executing projects or getting approvals, Sivanandhan achieved these with great speed. This was because of his mobilization skills that come through good networks.

★ TIPS FOR WORKING WITH ALLIES AND FRIENDS ★

1. Network: It is important to have a good network of friends.

2. Organize meetings: Gather regular information from your team.

3. Use your intelligence: It is important to distinguish between right and wrong.

4. Cultivate informers: They are your key to creating strategy.

5. Help your friends: You need to help your allies when they are in need.

The Leader in Me

Notes

About the Authors

Dr Radhakrishnan Pillai is from the University of Mumbai. He is a trainer, researcher, author and teacher on leadership. His first book, *Corporate Chanakya*, created records in the management books category. Apart from being a popular bestseller, the book has also been considered for academic research in educational institutions across the globe. Having trained and mentored thousands of leaders, Dr Pillai is well-known for making Chanakya popular as a management and leadership guru.

D Sivanandhan has practiced leadership in the police force for over 35 years in life-threatening situations. He began his professional life as an assistant professor of Economics at Madras University, but joined the Indian Police Service (IPS) in 1976. His key postings include a six-year stint at the Intelligence Bureau (1987–93), first as DCP, and then as Deputy Director. During 1995–98, he led the police in anti-Naxal operations as Deputy SP – Deputy IGP, Nagpur Range. His most significant achievement is often considered to be during his posting as Joint CP (Crime), Mumbai (July 1998–March 2001), when under his strategic leadership, the police succeeded in breaking the hegemony of the underworld over the city. Apart from his leadership skills, Sivanandhan is also known for his keen interest and contribution to the welfare of the police force. He was actively involved in building schools for police children in Naxal strongholds such as Gadchiroli and Chandrapur. Subsequently, as CP – Thane City (February 2005–May 2008), he created the Thane Police School, a world-class institution to impart education to the children of policemen as well as other citizens. He has also been involved in various health initiatives for the police, such as building hospitals and gymnasiums, organizing health check-ups and yoga classes and so on. After the Mumbai terror attack on November 26, 2008, Sivanandhan took over as Commissioner of Police – Mumbai (June 2009– May 2010). During this period, he revamped the city's security infrastructure to ensure better preparedness for threats like terror attacks. As Director General Police of Maharashtra state (May 2010–March 2011), he successfully led a force of over 2.5 lakh policemen and policewomen. After his retirement in 2011, he worked as part of the Prime Minister's Office (PMO) and is currently working for the Reserve Bank of India. Sivanandhan and his leadership style have been much discussed and debated in the media. His strategies to tackle criminals have inspired Bollywood films. His situational leadership strategies have been used as case studies in academic institutions in India and abroad.

INVITE

Radhakrishnan Pillai and D Sivanandhan to conduct a session on Chanakya's 7 secrets of leadership in your organization.

Write to: *info@ciplmumbai.in* OR *Sourav@seventeenevents.com*

OR

Call: +91-9819993300, 9820941012, 022-26206195

OR

Visit: *www.seventeenevents.com*

TO KNOW MORE ABOUT

SECURUS 🛡 FIRST

D Sivanandhan, visit: *www.securusfirst.com*

Radhakrishnan Pillai, visit: *www.ciplmumbai.in*

TO GET MORE INFORMATION ABOUT

The management film *Chanakya Speaks – The 7 pillars for success in business* and the training kit, 'Chanakya in You', visit: *www.chanakyaspeaks.in*

CHANAKYA's CHAKRAVYUH

(A financial game based on Arthashastra)
www.chanakyaschakkravyuh.com
Call: +917738688532